PRAISE FOR

THE WORSHIP WARRIOR

The Lord is downloading information, strategy, commands and provision to His people at an unprecedented rate. *The Worship Warrior* is a rich, poetic visual—a blueprint—of how to accomplish your destiny by making God more real than any person or circumstance so that His will be done upon Earth.

JAIME LYN BAUER
ACTRESS, INTERCESSOR

I respect Chuck Pierce for his passion to be on the cutting edge of what God is revealing to His Church. In *The Worship Warrior*, Chuck gives us a blueprint for worship that will cast the net for the harvest of the nations.

MIKE BICKLE
DIRECTOR, INTERNATIONAL HOUSE OF PRAYER IN KANSAS CITY

I'm convinced the message of *The Worship Warrior* is the number one message God wants the Church to hear in this age of both extraordinary challenge and incredible opportunity. History's greatest harvest is soon to happen, and worship will be at the heart of it.

DR. DICK EASTMAN
INTERNATIONAL PRESIDENT, EVERY HOME FOR CHRIST

The church struggles today to understand the vital link between worship and spiritual warfare. Some Christians want to focus all their attention on fighting demons, while others actually propose that we totally ignore our spiritual enemies and worship all the time to see victory. A balance is needed, and I believe Chuck Pierce and John Dickson have tapped into the heart of God on this strategic issue.

J. LEE GRADY
EDITOR, *CHARISMA* MAGAZINE

The life of King David has always impressed me. He was Israel's most loved king and greatest warrior. However, what is most remembered is that David had a heart after God's own heart. In other words, David was a worshiper. It was his devotion to worship that made him a great king and warrior. In *The Worship Warrior*, Chuck Pierce and John Dickson give us fresh insight into this marvelous relationship of worship and warfare. For the days ahead, we must learn how to ascend first in worship, receiving strength, wisdom and courage, and then descend into the battle to push back the gates of hell and establish His Kingdom.

DUTCH SHEETS
AUTHOR, *INTERCESSORY PRAYER*

This book is going to print precisely at a time when the Body of Christ in America is at war. There's nothing more dangerous, when facing a frontal assault, than to be found living a civilian lifestyle. The spiritual alertness and focus to which this book calls us is absolutely critical in this hour. *The Worship Warrior* will help establish you before the throne, from which vantage you will watch God avenge you of your enemies.

BOB SORGE
AUTHOR, *SECRETS OF THE SECRET PLACE*

In *The Worship Warrior*, the voice of King David is released to this generation through the clear prophetic teaching of Chuck Pierce and John Dickson. In this hour where spiritual battle is increasingly manifested in the natural realm, the people of God must be equipped to become steadfast, unmovable, persevering worshipers who know how to move into corporate prayer that prevails. May the Lord use this book to release David's heart as a "corporate David" rises up in this chosen generation.

ROBERT STEARNS
EXECUTIVE DIRECTOR, EAGLES WINGS, NEW YORK

You hold in your hands a weapon of warfare to be wielded only by the worshipful. It will draw you near to Him in pursuit of intimate relationship; yet you will find it to be a call to war. Its sound will compel you to enter the battle that will release the harvest in which God will be glorified and Satan defeated. Chuck Pierce has uniquely combined sound scriptural teaching on worship and spiritual warfare with personal experience and the outflow of his own personal anointing as a worshipful singer and songwriter. This book will change your life—as you become a worshipful warrior!

TOMMY TENNEY
AUTHOR, *THE GOD CHASERS*

THE WORSHIP WARRIOR

CHUCK D. PIERCE
WITH
JOHN DICKSON

Regal

From Gospel Light
Ventura, California, U.S.A.

Published by Regal
From Gospel Light
Ventura, California, U.S.A.
www.regalbooks.com
Printed in the U.S.A.

Library of Congress Cataloging-in-Publication Data
Pierce, Chuck D., 1953–
   The worship warrior / Chuck D. Pierce with John Dickson.
      p. cm.
   Includes bibliographical references and index.
   ISBN 0-8307-3056-7
   1. God—Worship and love. 2. Spiritual warfare. I. Dickson, John,
1951– II. Title.
   BV4817 .P54 2002
      243—dc21   2002012098

   12   13   14   15   16   17   18   19   20   /   12   11   10   09   08

Rights for publishing this book outside the U.S.A. or in non-English languages are administered by Gospel Light Worldwide, an international not-for-profit ministry. For additional information, please visit www.glww.org, email info@glww.org, or write to Gospel Light Worldwide, 1957 Eastman Avenue, Ventura, CA 93003, U.S.A.

CONTENTS

WORSHIP
THE

WARRIOR

FOREWORD

My friend Charles Doolittle and about 20 intercessors gathered not long ago in a Studio City, California, home. "Let us enter the Throne Room and receive our marching orders," Charles prayed. "Let us worship God and enter into the battle." Another member of the group added, "There is a fresh sound of God. Let us hear that sound!"

Worship and warfare? Enter the Throne Room? A sound of God? A casual observer might have thought Charles and his fellow intercessors had uttered malapropisms. But nothing could be further from the truth. Indeed, the members of this group of believers, who regularly intercede for the entertainment industry in Hollywood, are worship warriors.

I too have often experienced the reality of these power twins of the Spirit. In 2000, Will Ford, Lou Engle, myself and 30 or so other intercessors carried a 200-year-old, formerly slave-owned kettle across northeast America, using it as a catalyst for intercessory worship and warfare. To us it symbolized the prayer bowls in heaven (see Rev. 8:3-5), as we filled it with prayer and praise for revival in America.

I have stood with a U.S. senator in the rotunda of the U.S. Capitol, mixing prayer and praise in order to break the strongholds of darkness and release the government of God over America. The exalting of the Lord in worship, mixed with the overcoming force of intercession, was thrilling to experience.

What happened in that Studio City home, on the Kettle Tour and in the U.S. Capitol is beginning to occur across the nation and around the world as we enter a pivotal time of intense spiritual warfare. Yes, intercession thrives, but prayer warriors are beginning to understand the role of worship in their warfare.

Chuck Pierce and John Dickson have written this book to introduce you to this major shift in worship that is happening in the Body of Christ today. Some of the words and concepts may not be familiar, but stick with Pierce and Dickson. You will see that this call for us to become strategic worship warriors is biblical and imperative. We must integrate it into the fabric of the Church if we want to see God's destiny fulfilled in our individual and corporate lives.

I will leave the details for Chuck and John to explain; instead, I will use the remaining space in this foreword to give you a word of encouragement and a call to passionate worship.

There is a fresh sound of God in this day. It is filled with glory and releases passion. Our everyday lives give us ample opportunities to develop it. We do not need to be at church or in a prayer meeting. We can be soccer moms en route to practice, lawyers in between briefs or plumbers reaching for a wrench. Wherever we are and whatever we do, we can worship. We were made to honor and glorify God our creator, and we are destined to war. Do not be deterred by adverse circumstances or by mundane situations. Rather, be filled with the good things of the Lord. We are in love with Jesus, and we are extravagant, unquench-able, uncommon, unstoppable, determined and passionate worshipers.

In worship, we need to have the passion of a Charles Wesley. Matt Redman tells the story:

> The year is 1744. Hymn writer Charles Wesley is in Leads, England, holding a prayer meeting in an upstairs room. Suddenly there is a creak in the floor-boards, followed by a massive crack, and the whole floor collapses. All 100 people crash right through the ceiling into the room below. The place is in chaos—some are screaming, some are crying, some just sit in shock. But as the dust settles, Wesley, wounded and lying in a heap, cries out, "Fear not! The Lord is with us; our lives are all safe." And then he breaks out into the doxology: "Praise God, from whom all blessings flow"—perhaps a bizarre choice of songs considering what has just happened! But here's the point: While everyone else was still licking their wounds, the heart of this unstoppable worshipper was responding with unshakable praise.[1]

This is the type of worshiper who will become an effec-tive warrior.

Dutch Sheets
Senior Pastor
Springs Harvest Fellowship
Colorado Springs, CO

Note

1. Matt Redman, *The Unquenchable Worshipper* (Ventura, CA: Regal Books, 2001), p. 74.

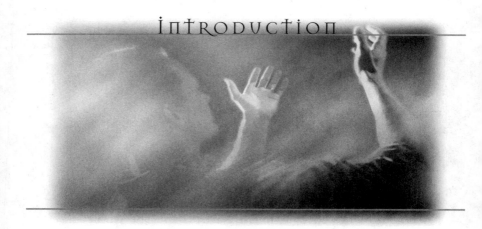

What Does Worship Have to Do with War?

Light overpowers darkness, truth alone prevails hurt
Death has no power when the enemy assails.
Through the eyes of the spirit the battle rages on
Engaged in relentless war we intercede, stand firm and strong.
Equipped for end-time battle clad in armor of the flesh
No holes or tares are seen, woven mighty metal mesh.
Arms gripped together . . . vice-locked, no space
Like a giant wall of iron we move as one to take our place.
Immovable, undefeatable, an army bold and strong
Worshiping warriors engaged in battle raise the victorious war song.

Hear the gatekeepers give a shout vigilant watchmen on the wall
Protecting holy ground as the trumpet sounds the call.
Arise ye men of Zion, ye Samurai of the King
Lift high His royal banner for we win and victory rings.
BEV SMITH, *THE BATTLE*

When we hear the word "worship," many of us think of singing three or four hymns in a Sunday-morning church service. Some picture quiet times or Bible studies. A few visualize prayer.

The word "warrior," on the other hand, easily evokes images of a person in the heat of combat. Perhaps we imagine Russell Crowe in the movie *Gladiator* or envision army troops on the front lines in Afghanistan. Maybe we think of a person who battles in the loosely defined "wars" against social nemeses such as poverty, prejudice and injustice. Perhaps, as believers, we recall C. Peter Wagner's call to become strategic prayer warriors.

While the words "worship" and "war" are familiar, they nonetheless produce extreme and opposing emotions—seldom do we see the two work in tandem. As servants of God, we know we are to worship Him. We also know that we fight in a spiritual battle. But a close look at the Bible reveals much about God's plan for worship in war.

So exactly how do these two fit together?

THE WORSHIP WARS

Every war has a cause or purpose. Napoleon marched in quest of territory—he hoped that France would rule Europe. Lenin and Stalin spread their communist dogma with expectations of dominating Eastern Europe and beyond—they sought to transform what people thought and how they lived. The United States attacked Iraq in Desert Storm to protect oil interests and support allies in the region—we wanted to liberate Kuwait.

These physical and ideological skirmishes were played out on Earth, but a greater war is also afoot. The larger battle is in the spiritual dimension, yet fought both on Earth and in the heavenlies. In the natural, we cannot see this conflict of good versus evil. But God, even though He could win on His own, has chosen us as His warriors.

Lucifer's Plot

Worship is at the center of this great spiritual war. It has always been about worship, fought with worship and will be won through worship.

Let me explain. Lucifer (also known as the devil or Satan) picked a fight with God. The Bible does not make clear exactly when this happened, but it certainly occurred before Adam and Eve ate the forbidden fruit and, tempted by the promise to be like God, introduced sin to the world (see Gen. 3:1-4).

We know from Ezekiel 28:12-19 that in that time cherubs or angels, of which Lucifer was one, had access to the holy mountain or Throne Room of heaven—where God is seated. Some theologians think that Lucifer actually led the angels as they worshiped the Creator. If this is true, Lucifer, whose heart was "lifted up because of his beauty" (v. 17), apparently decided that he no longer wanted to be a worshiper; instead, he wanted to be worshiped. His wisdom was corrupted because of his brightness. Full of pride, he was cast down, and he convinced many angels to join him in rebellion against God.

Thus, the worship wars were on.

WORSHIP AND THE WARRIOR

We usually render worship in adoration toward God and associate it with good, uplifting, even ecstatic feelings. Worship is often focused upward and can embody the qualities of holiness, reverence and awe. We see ourselves as givers and God as the recipient.

Warring, on the other hand, involves taking a stand, overcoming a threat, invading territory or conquering an enemy. In war we often view ourselves as defenders against a dangerous force or sustainers of righteousness and truth. This is true in physical and spiritual conflicts.

In the physical, or earthly, realm we tend to worship the human heroes of battle and add God as an afterthought. The typical scenario does not include worship as part of the battle plan; instead, worship comes in the form of thanksgiving *after a victory*. In spiritual conquests, the Almighty gets all of the praise, but we still see warfare and worship as two separate acts.

Our understanding needs to expand. God is calling us to bridge worship and warfare. When we read the Bible, we find that God instructs us to *ascend* into the Throne Room in heaven, be *clothed* in His authority and *descend* in war. There is a *sound* of heaven that enables us to recognize, embrace and advance through this process. It moves us toward victory in accomplishing God's will on Earth. I explain each of these elements in this book.

A Fresh Approach

God is calling us to be worship warriors!

For many Christians, this is a new concept. We have come to understand how we can take authority over demons, territories and sin of all types, in the name of Jesus. We know how our prayers affect what happens not only on Earth, but also in the heavenlies. We have been good students of the principles of spiritual warfare.

This is all good. But God is calling us to do more.

In *The Future War of the Church*, Rebecca Wagner Sytsema and I describe a coming battle. We show how there will be a time of increased struggle and, ultimately, prophetic fulfillment. As the Church approaches this future war, we need to be prepared. We must fully comprehend the place of worship. As we battle against the enemies of darkness, we need to grasp the authority God has given us. We must become worship warriors.

A Transformation of Worship

Is worship singing? Is it praying? Is it demonstrating outwardly our love of God by using our bodies? Do we need music in order to worship? Does our environment have to be quiet? Can we worship at work or while shopping? Can we worship at our child's piano recital? Can we praise God while in a carpool on the way to work?

Worship comes in all of these forms and places and in many more. Many of us have embraced a lifestyle of worship in which we express our praise of God not only in church but also in the routine of our daily lives. This is excellent and right. However, our adoration and our intimate quest to know God should never stop us short of exercising His will on Earth. This means worship is more than a song or a meditation; but what is this more?

In the future, will we worship like Moses and Deborah? Will Daniel become our key model of worship? Can we agonize like Jesus did in Gethsemane and still worship? Can we know when to work like Martha and when to submit like Mary? Will worship change drastically in corporate settings? Will we be bold to worship in public places? Will the enemy recognize our anointing after we have been in God's presence?

What will worship look like in the future?

A Rising Tide

In recent days, John Dickson and I have seen a powerful shift in worship. That is why we have expanded upon the message of *The Future War of the Church* and penned the book you now hold in your hands. I (Chuck) have written in first person and have liberally quoted John where his insights have been so keen. But John has also contributed immensely to the concepts and truths in every chapter, even in places where he is not credited.

We want to lay before you the principles we have learned. We seek to show you how as believers we can engage in and win this spiritual conflict. We desire to stir up a sense of excitement among Christians everywhere.

As you read, listen for God's voice. You will be encouraged to learn what happens both in the heavenlies and on Earth—the two realms where the battle unfolds—when as a congregation of believers we worship as warriors.

THE CALLING OF GOD

God is pursuing His people. The Spirit of the Lord is calling us to worship. God is releasing a sound from heaven that is being embraced by people all over the world. The call causes us to draw near to Him and to each other. The sound causes us to go to war. We must manifest on Earth what God says in heaven.

God does not play favorites. Everyone can embrace this call to become a worship warrior. If we believe in Jesus, we are automatically enlisted in His army.

Mark Twain once said, "God loves common people. That's why He made so many of us."[1] God is not calling only ministers to a lifestyle of worship; He is also calling everyday people. In biblical times, He called olive pickers, shepherds, fishermen, tax collectors, young people and many others. The apostle Paul said, "Not many wise according to the flesh, not many mighty, not many noble, are called" (1 Cor. 1:26).

The same is true today. It is just us: carpenters, computer programmers, secretaries, bus drivers, farmers and the like. Yes, there are some lawyers, CEOs and Harvard graduates, too. But before God we are one, and all become common, no matter our profession or place in society. It is therefore everyday people who fill the ranks in God's army of worshipers. He calls us from our everyday lives to be separated out and holy unto Him.

ENTER THE BATTLE

Worship warriors arise! Worship Warriors of every generation, young and old, connect and stand. This is the time to worship, enter boldly into the Throne Room, be clothed with favor and go to war. The sound is being released. Listen to it. Enter the battle. Release the harvest!

Note

1. Mark Twain [Samuel Clemens], *Letters from the Earth* (New York: Perennial Library, Harper and Row, Publishers, 1938), n.p.

CHAPTER
I

A NEW THING

I've been bought with a price
I've been redeemed by the blood of the Lamb
I've got the love of the Father and His Spirit living in me
Now I'm having done with my old ways
And I'm looking ahead to some new days
And I'm leaving behind my previous destiny

Now I'm ready to get up, show up, stand up and speak up
Raise up a howl, put my hand to the plow
I won't back down, back up, quit or let my love grow cold
I'm finished with tame faith, smooth knees, small dreams
No more mundane living or chinchy giving
I've grabbed a hold the hem of His garment and I won't let go
JOHN DICKSON, GET UP!

Hang a banana on a string in a cage full of apes, with stairs under the banana. Before long, an ape will go to the stairs and start to climb toward the banana. As soon as he touches the stairs, spray all of the apes with cold water.

After awhile, another ape will make an attempt, but the result will be the same—all the apes will be sprayed with cold water. This should continue through several more attempts. Pretty soon, when another ape tries to climb the stairs, the other apes will all try to prevent it.

Now, turn off the cold water. Remove one ape from the cage and replace it with a new one. The new ape will see the banana and want to climb the stairs. To his horror, all of the other apes will attack him. After another attempt and attack, he'll know that if he tries to climb the stairs, he will be assaulted.

Next, remove another of the original five apes and replace it with a new one. The newcomer will go to the stairs and be attacked. The previous newcomer will take part in the punishment.

Replace a third original ape with a new one. The new one will make it to the stairs and be attacked as well. Two of the four apes that beat him will have no idea why they were not permitted to climb the stairs, or why they are participating in the beating of the newest ape.

After replacing the fourth and fifth original apes, all the apes, which have been sprayed with cold water, will have been replaced. Nevertheless, no ape will ever again approach the stairs. Why not?

Because that's the way they've always done it, and that's the way it's always been around here.[1]

I love this story! It vividly illustrates a point I want to make. How many times has someone said to you, "We do such-and-such this way because we have always done it this way"? We get going in one direction and no matter how much the world around us changes, we keep doing the same thing over and over again.

This "thing" can be the way we fold our clothes, the food we eat, the route we drive to work or any of a zillion other everyday acts. A method or measurement works when it is first done, but then we repeat it and eventually transfer it from generation to generation. No one ever questions the act or considers a more creative or effective approach because "it was good enough for my grandfather, so it is good enough for me." In other words, we have always done it that way.

We are guilty of this habit in the Church, too. We have our customs, rituals and regimens when it comes to preaching, membership, leadership, prayer and so many other factors—*including worship*. There is nothing wrong with common sacraments in and of themselves, but too often what were once fresh expressions of faith become lifeless traditions.

Even in "contemporary" churches we have established new conventions and often repeat them. We sing the same songs, turn the lights down low or raise our hands. These started out as authentic acts, and some continue to spark vibrant ministry, but many are similar to a sailboat. The captain will raise and maneuver the sail, so it catches the fullness of the wind and the boat builds up speed. When the wind changes direction, the sail will remain full and the boat will zip along for quite some time because of the momentum. If the sail is not tilted with the wind, however, the boat will slow down and soon lie motionless, dead in the water. The key is to adjust the sail at just the right moment so that the wind continues to push the boat forward at full thrust.

When it comes to worship, we need to see what God is doing that is new.

A NEW SEASON

When God says, "I am doing a new thing," He does not neces-sarily mean something that He has never done before.[2] In fact, while His purpose and promises never change (see Heb. 6:17), there are seasons, and His saving actions on behalf of His people

---

When God says,
"I am doing a new thing," He does
not necessarily mean something that
He has never done before.

---

have always had a variety of emphases, objectives and flavors. Look at what the Bible declares about His way of communicat-ing with His people: "In the past God spoke to our forefathers through the prophets at many times and in *various* ways" (Heb. 1:1-2, *NIV*, emphasis added).

God's View of "New"

I love prophets. They get us going one way and then turn us another way all in a matter of minutes. Consider the words of Isaiah: "Let me remind you of how God brought the people out of Egypt." The prophet has the Jewish people reflect upon a mar-velous miracle, but he does not let them tarry on that memory. "Forget that!" he quotes God. "For I'm going to do *a new thing,* do you not perceive it?" (see Isa. 43:18-19). Here God's new thing is a new act. However, the prophet uses the past as a reference point to steer His people forward. God does the same for us today. He uses past events in our lives to prod us to the next level. He is doing that with worship right now.

Consider your great moments with God. When was the last incredible meeting time you had with the Lord? Was it your day of salvation? How about that time when God met you and healed you? Or was it when He brought your wayward child back into the fold?

We can praise God for each blessing, but we cannot rest our hope in any of them. Biblical faith does not relegate God to yesterday. If we expect God to act today only in the ways He has acted in the past, we could miss what He is doing now to bring us into a new place. God's actions will always be biblical—He never wavers from that foundation—but that does not mean they will not vary.

The Start of a New Thing

When the Lord launches a new thing, He builds new relationships with us. In fact, such freshness of relationship is the cornerstone of each new season and each spiritual breakthrough. However, if there is to be new relationship we must open our

When the Lord launches a new thing, He builds new relationships with us.

hearts. That is where worship comes in and why it is so important. Through worship we have intimate contact with God and unlock His blessings. As we come close to Him in true worship, He will renew and reshape our hearts and we will see His heart.

Another aspect of the new is death. We must die to something for new life to come forth. For instance, when we die to our old methods of worshiping God, newness of life begins to spring forth in our hearts and on Earth. When we worship in a new way, we conceive. And when we conceive, we bring forth what God wants for this hour and time.

When God does a new thing, we go from one place to another. We move from strength to strength, faith to faith and glory to glory. Notice that we do not dwell in our current strength or faith or glory; rather, we go forward just as the Israelites did. We move from one strength to another, from one faith to another and from one glory to another. We cannot do this on our own, but through worship God can carry us there.

In a way, God progressively takes us from one new thing to another, but how do we know what the new thing is that God wants and when we are to move into that which is new?

A NEW PLACE

God not only does new things in the heavenlies, but He also brings what is new into our individual lives. These new things can be small or big. They can be tweaks of attitudes or directions to new paths that will forever change the courses of our lives. The big new things can occur quickly and often. One happened to me on December 31, 1983. Here is my story.

I had been praying intensely for the Church in the Soviet bloc, particularly what then was still the Soviet Union. As I prayed, I saw the Church strapped down with oppression. I observed the Body of Christ of that nation and counted seven straps holding it from coming into the influence the Lord wanted it to have. The Spirit of God spoke to me and said, "I want the straps cut."

I had an incredible prayer time that night and went to bed ready to start a new year. Then, sometime after midnight, I awakened and the Spirit of God visited and spoke to me. He began to give me a strategy of how He was going to free the Church in the Soviet Union. He said "change of leadership" and showed me that when the third leader came into power in the Soviet Union the Church would have an open window to advance. That night I spent approximately two hours with the Lord and wrote down everything He said to me.

The next morning I got up and at breakfast told my wife, Pam, about my visitation. After giving her the details, I announced: "I must be called to the Soviet Union."

At that time, we were administrators of the second largest children's home in Texas. I never will forget her response: "You might be called to the Soviet Union, but I'm not. As a matter of fact, I was walking across the campus and the Spirit of God spoke to me that He is going to heal my body and I am going to get pregnant."

Pam then added, "This is going to be an interesting walk with you called to the Soviet Union and me getting pregnant."

The Meaning of Following

With two such clear, but contrasting words from God, we knew that we had to seek the Lord's direction concerning our future. In my quiet time that night, the Spirit of God quickened two words to me: "Follow me." Pam and I agreed to study the principle of following God as it is declared in the Word of God.

As we began our study in the Old Testament, we looked at the life of Abraham. He was called out of one form of worship in Ur of the Chaldees—the worship of Molech, which is part of the Queen of Heaven system—*to follow* after a Holy God. This brought Abraham into a blessing-filled covenant agreement with God.

After reading Genesis 12 and 15, Pam and I saw that we could enjoy the same blessings Abraham enjoyed because as believers we are grafted into the same covenant. We realized that if we were to see our Abraham-like blessings manifested we would have to follow God and worship Him in a new way. Just as Abraham left the familiarity and comfort of Ur, we would have to be willing to give up our traditions.

In our study, we also noticed a pattern set by Jesus when He called His disciples. They were to leave their homes, careers, families, friends and old forms of religious practice, and they were to follow Him. Some of the disciples had attended temple often; others knew very little about worship.

Jesus set an example of a new thing in worship. He went directly to the Father on their behalf and told them that they had access to the Father's will for their lives. This clearly sets forth the biblical relationship between *going* and *worship* that unlocks a person's destiny.

As we studied the model of Jesus, the Lord quickened these words to me; "If you will learn to *follow me*, you will *see revival*." "Revival" means to restore to life that which has been diverted into a process of death. I thought of Pam's womb, and I also thought of the Church in the Soviet Union. Both would see revival.

Signs Along the Way

Pam and I knew we were hearing from God, but we still did not know all of the details. One night we were on our way to a prayer meeting at a Baptist church when I stopped for gas. As we began to drive away from the service station, we saw a large truck that had two words written on its back side: FOLLOW ME. I knew this was a sign from the Lord and followed the truck. When I got closer I could read the smaller lettering: Harpool Incorporated, Denton, Texas. Pam got the strangest look on her face and explained, "I am reading a book called *Peace, Prosperity and the Holocaust* by Dave Hunt. The book is not specifically about the Soviet Union, but it is dedicated to a missions group that is located in Denton, Texas, that works in the Soviet Union."

That missions group was Mission Possible Foundation, Inc. I made a quick decision to take vacation time the following week so that I could visit the organization's leaders to share with them the insights about the Soviet Union that I was receiving from the Holy Spirit.

Worship in Spirit and in Truth

Mission Possible's leaders readily received me and listened to the concerns of my heart. That night Pam and I went to a conference hosted by James Robison. God used the worship time to build up this new thing He was doing in our lives.

As we worshiped God, Pam and I expressed ourselves in different ways. I was exuberant, filled with incredible joy, waving my hands because of the liberation God had brought into my life.

> I only know that God has set me free and I cannot keep myself from responding to that freedom.

Pam, on the other hand, clearly understood the biblical principles of worship but was more reserved in how she expressed herself to the Lord. She worshiped in *word*, and I worshiped in *spirit*. That night I saw it this way: since we were (and still are) married, we stood and worshiped as one. We worshiped in Spirit and in truth, and whenever, as believers, we do that, we actually enter into the reality of God's purposes.

Pam did not exactly see it the same way as I did. On the way home that night, she made a curious observation: "I only see two places in the New Testament where it talks about raising hands. You are so expressive in your worship that it has created problems for us."

I quickly replied, "I don't really care if the principle of raising hands is only in the concordance of the Bible. I only know that God has set me free and I cannot keep myself from responding to that freedom."

Increasing the tension between the two of us, I then added, "If you get as desperate as I once was to allow God to do things that need to be done, you'll probably express yourself in worship a different way."

Healing in Worship

The next day we returned to the conference and I felt the presence of God surround us. I looked over at my wife, and she had both hands in the air and was waving them. I gently asked, "What is happening with you?" Amidst the tears that were streaming down her face she said, "The Lord is healing me!"

The presence of God began to flow down her body. She describes it as something similar to hot oil going through her veins. God's power actually pushed the clots (that had resulted from endometriosis) from her uterus and out of her body.

Two weeks later, Pam became pregnant. Then she got pregnant again and again and again and again! The power of God had been released in her body as she worshiped God in a whole new way.

I eventually ended up serving as the executive director of the missions agency that was working in the Soviet Union. I remained a part of that organization until those straps were removed from the Church in the Soviet Union and there was a window for evangelism to advance.

Pam and I had followed God and had learned to worship in a new way. We had come into a new level of unity in our marriage. Worship had broken the power of barrenness in our lives. God's anointing had broken the yoke. If we had done things the way we had always done them, we would have never seen breakthrough to new things God wanted done in our lives.

A NEW THING IN WORSHIP

God is doing a new thing in worship. This is happening not only in individual lives, but in the whole Church. Over the ages worship itself has shifted, grown and blossomed. From the Georgian chants of the fourth century to Wesley's hymns of the eighteenth century, there have been many variations. In the twentieth century alone we spanned a full spectrum from George Beverley Shea's

---

When God does a new thing,
He makes a fresh sound that we can
hear in the earthly realm.

---

gospel tunes to the Vineyard's deep soaking in the presence of God to Mike Bickle's intensive 24-hour-a-day model at his International House of Prayer in Kansas City, Missouri.

As we have turned the corner into the new millennium, we are seeing another momentous shift in worship, which may be related to God's redemptive work in our time and pivotal in the spiritual battle both on Earth and in the heavenlies. We are advancing to an intimate, strategic, warring worship.

When God does a new thing, He makes a fresh sound that we can hear in the earthly realm. Moreover, I believe that this fresh sound is also rising up into heaven.

> Thus says the LORD, who makes a way in the sea and a path through the mighty waters, who brings forth the chariot and horse, the army and the power (they shall lie down together, they shall not rise; they are extinguished, they are quenched like a wick): "Do not remember the former things, nor consider the things of old. Behold, I will do a new thing, now it shall spring forth; shall you not know it? I will even make a road in the wilderness and rivers in the desert" (Isa. 43:16-19).

Put aside the ways things have always been done. Open up to the new things of God. Listen for His sound. Get up! Ascend to the Throne Room of God. Receive His anointing and advance into strategic, warring worship.

Notes

1. "That's the Way We've Always Done It," *Murphy in the Morning*. http://www.murphyinthemorning.com/banana.htm (accessed July 11, 2002).
2. *The New Strong's Exhaustive Concordance of the Bible*, s.v. "kainos." There are actually four Greek words for "new": *agnaaphos* (unsmoothed), *kainos* (fresh), *neos* (young) and *prosphatos* (newly slain or recent). Kainos conveys new in form or quality, whereas neos implies newness in time. To understand what God is doing that is new in worship we should use kainos—it is new in form and quality.

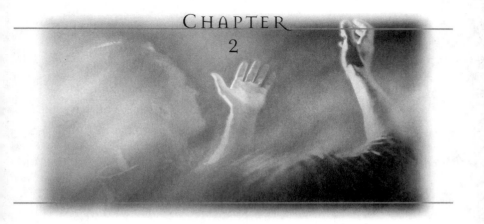

GOING WHERE GOD IS

Evangelist and pastor Greg Laurie has identified the prevailing problem all humans face. "We each have a hole in our heart, a spiritual vacuum deep within our soul—a 'God-shaped blank.'"[1] Some Christians have called this a God-shaped void. In this book, John Dickson and I want to draw that void into the transforming presence of the holy God. In His hands, we become like clay and can be shaped in His image. Once we have been molded into the image of our holy God, then we can accomplish the purpose for which He created us.

What does worship have to do with this? Worship is the human response to the perceived presence of a divine being. This must be a presence that transcends normal human activity. We are made to worship. As we worship, we move in a realm of faith that pleases God.

The LORD reigns; let the peoples tremble! He dwells between the cherubim; let the earth be moved! The LORD is great in Zion, and He is high above all the peoples. Let them praise Your great and awesome name—He is holy. The King's strength also loves justice; You have established equity; You have executed justice and righteousness in Jacob. Exalt the LORD our God, and worship at His footstool—He is holy (Ps. 99:1-5).

THE HISTORY OF WORSHIP

When we worship we bow down or stoop before someone in an act of submission or reverence. Worship actually means to make oneself low. It is the opposite of self-exaltation. Therefore, to exalt the Lord actually means for us to fall at His feet and honor Him for who He is in our lives. The Bible tells us that God is high above all people. That means that when we worship, we must come to the place where God is.

If we are believers and have accepted Jesus as the Lord of our lives, we know that we are His temples and His Spirit dwells within us. We know that God descended to the earthly realm and God made Himself known through His Son, Jesus.

We know that when Jesus rose from the grave He overcame death and hell. We know Jesus ascended to heaven, and in His ascent He gave gifts to mankind. We also know He left the Holy Spirit here on Earth to fill our human spirits (that void) and connect us with the heavenly realm where He sits at the Father's right hand. We know that Jesus is our mediator. On our behalf, He boldly goes before our holy Father in the Throne Room.

The act of worship satisfies both our desire to honor God and His desire for us to be fulfilled. True worship must have a singular focus on the object that is being worshiped. Everything else must be set aside, so the worshiper can come face-to-face with the object of veneration. As believers, we must move past angels, saints, shrines, relics, religious paraphernalia, spouses, children, other believers, friends, powers and authorities and bow low. If we are to accomplish God's purposes in our day, we must present ourselves to Him.

Picture your favorite dog. He or she likely comes up to you, affectionately licks your hand and, with warm eyes, in effect says: "I'm here to serve you. You are the most important person in my life. I am willing to obey your every command. Throw a stick, and I will fetch it. Command me to go into that cold water, and I will gladly go and retrieve."

This is how we should be when we worship God.

Hide or Seek—Our Choice

Imagine walking, talking and communing with the Spirit of God all day long. That is how it was with Adam and Eve in the Garden. Their communion was so powerful that work and worship became one.

This perfect communion caused the Garden to prosper. This was God's ultimate plan. Satan hated this perfect communion. He knows the power we have in the earthly realm when we truly walk and talk with the Lord. Therefore, he had to find a way to interrupt the prosperity of the Garden. He had to accuse God over His word, defy the Holy Spirit and cause Eve to question what God had said. This questioning and relying upon her own reasoning was really the first deviation from true worship.

Reasoning always leads to disobedience. Therefore, Adam left the true plan of worship and disobeyed God. Once both man and woman were disconnected from this perfect communion, they began to recognize things they never saw before.

Genesis 3:8 records what happened next. Adam and Eve "heard the sound of the LORD God walking in the garden . . . [and]

hid themselves from the presence of the LORD." We find this same idea of hiding ourselves from God in Revelation 6:16, but there it applies to the condition of mankind unless we are reconciled back to God via worship.

God prefers that we come before Him boldly, and walk and talk with Him.

Hiding is so contrary to what God wants us to do. He prefers that we come before Him boldly, and walk and talk with Him. The question the Lord asked Adam is chilling: "Where are you?" (Gen. 3:9). I am sure God is asking many of us this question today. Where are we?

The Worship War on Earth
The Lord responded to how His plan of communion and worship had been interrupted. He cursed the serpent and prophesied to the woman, promising her that her seed would crush the serpent's head. He then cursed the ground and told Adam that he would now have to work in the midst of that which He had cursed. Before then, Adam had worshiped and worked. Now, he would sweat and toil.

As we read on in Genesis, we find that after the Fall worship becomes the biggest contention between mankind and God. In Genesis 4, Abel worshiped in a way that pleased God. Cain, on the other hand, wanted to worship in his own way. When we refuse to shift and worship God the way He longs to be worshiped, we make the same mistake Cain made.

Out of God's Presence

Notice, when Cain worshiped the way he wanted to worship, this resulted in contention, jealousy, competition, self-exaltation, hatred, envy and eventually murder. However, we find another disastrous pattern recorded in Genesis 4:16: "Then Cain went out from the presence of the LORD."

Being out from under the presence of God is probably the scariest thing I can think of. When we do not worship the way the Lord wants us to worship and the way He is worthy of being worshiped, we begin to create our own society. This man-made society is built around our own ideas and philosophies. Such a system breeds idolatry.

In Nod, Cain and his wife began to bear children. One child built a city "out from the presence of God." Others dwelt in tents and had livestock. This means that the whole agricultural system was out from the presence of the Lord. Jubal was the father of all of those who played the harp and flute. This means that music was out from the presence of the Lord. There was teaching of every craftsman in bronze and iron. This means that manufacturing and industry was out from the presence of the Lord.

Five generations later we read that Lamech, a descendant of Cain, kills a man (see Gen. 4:23). When we are out from the presence of the Lord, iniquitous patterns go from generation to generation. It also took generations for the proper worship of God to be restored:

> Adam knew his wife again, and she bore a son and named him Seth, "For God has appointed another seed for me instead of Abel, whom Cain killed" (Gen. 4:25).

God always has a righteous seed that He brings into a generation that is willing to restore His ultimate plan of worship and communion in the earth.

And as for Seth, to him also a son was born; and he named him Enosh. Then men began to call on the name of the LORD (Gen. 4:26).

Communion was restored. Men knew that the iniquitous patterns that operated in their city, in agriculture, industry and manufacturing could be changed if they would just worship the one true God.

WORSHIP ISSUES IN THIS SEASON

In every generation God has a remnant that longs to call out to Him. He has put that desire in the hearts of the people. The greatest desire in each of our hearts should be to walk fully restored in the earthly realm. When God created us before the

Whatever the issue in your life, the key is to worship a holy God.

foundation of Earth, He had an ultimate purpose for each one of us. There is something in each of us that says, "Lord, I want to fulfill Your desire for me during the time that I have here on Earth. Lord, when I see You, I want You to say to me, 'Well done, good and faithful servant.'" This is possible for each one of us.

Whatever the issue in your life, the key is to worship a holy God who created you and knows everything about you—your failures, shortcomings, insecurities, besetting sins and fears. Most important, He sits on His throne, omniscient, and says something like this: "I know your final destination, and I know how to get you from where you are now to where I want you to be. I know why I created you. If you'll worship Me, I will visit with you. I can tell you how to get untangled from the snares in your path and how to move forward. I can even reveal to you things to come that are pertinent to your life and world."

God may continue and say something that will startle you, words that are at the core of the message of this book. He might say something like this: "Come up into the Throne Room because this is where I will reveal Myself to you and share with you My desire for your life. These are days of restoration. I can restore your losses, but devote yourself to worshiping Me. My Son has given you access into My Throne Room. My Spirit can cause you to ascend and be enveloped by My love. Come up, so I might reveal Myself to you in a new way and cause My Word to become real to you, so it guides you in the path that I have set for you. *This is a time to worship.* If you will worship Me, you will know how to step forth into the path that I have for you in the days ahead. I will become one with you and overthrow every enemy that is in your path. *Ascend* into My Throne Room as you worship. *Descend* back to the harvest field and war for its release. I am ready for the harvest to come into My kingdom."

Ascend in worship? And descend in war? How can this be?

ASCEND: LET'S GO UP!

To ascend is to arise, climb, come up, get up, grow, increase, leap, light up, be raised, recover and restore. This comes from the Hebrew word *alah*. That is not the same word as the name of the Muslim god, Allah; rather, it is what Elohim, Adonai, Jehovah, Jesus—the one true God—calls upon us to do.

I find it interesting that God instructs His people to *alah* and worship. We are to boldly rise up, ascend, come into the Throne

Room and worship Him. When we follow this sequence, God's strategy of restoration is revealed to us.

One key biblical passage is Amos 9. This chapter is about the restoration of David's Tabernacle.

> The Lord GOD of hosts, He who touches the earth and it melts, and all who dwell there mourn; all of it shall swell like the River, and subside like the River of Egypt. He who builds His layers in the sky, and has founded His strata in the earth; who calls for the waters of the sea, and pours them out on the face of the earth—the LORD is His name (vv. 5-6).

We often overlook these verses, yet they are vital for us to understand. As we worship, we go up. The "layers" are like steps and stairs or upper chambers through the heavenlies that the Lord Jesus Christ has paved. It is a path that leads to the Throne Room.

These layers are like vaults that have keys. Jesus gives us the keys to unlock each vault as we ascend and draw near to Him in worship. Imagine each vault filled with treasure. Then we finally gain access to the Throne Room. These "layers in the sky" are also connected with the Lord's "strata in the earth." So as we ascend in worship and come into the Throne Room, Earth's strata begin to unlock. This planet we call home changes and receives the glory of God.

WHAT IS ASCENSION IN WORSHIP?

In a London cemetery is a grave and a headstone with a very unusual but beautiful wording. It was erected by the famous pastor Joseph Parker for his beloved wife. He could not bring himself to write the word "died"; instead, he chose the better word "ascended." Some time later, when he passed away, his friends had his headstone carved with the following inscription: "Joseph Parker, Born April 9, 1830, Ascended November 28, 1902."[2]

When we end our life cycle on Earth, we ascend to worship around the throne for eternity.

I like this. When we end our life cycle on Earth, we ascend to worship around the throne for eternity. But we have also seen that while still here in this temporary realm, we are supposed to be ascending. We have been given access to the Throne Room. This, of course, happens on a spiritual plane. Our bodies do not ascend, and we do not physically enter the Throne Room. However, just as we become one with Jesus in His ascension, so there are very real spiritual dynamics at work.

In Ephesians, the apostle Paul writes:

> Which He worked in Christ when He raised Him from the dead and seated Him at His right hand in the heavenly places, far above all principality and power and might and dominion, and every name that is named, not only in this age but also in that which is to come. And He put all things under His feet, and gave Him to be head over all things to the church, which is His body, the fullness of Him who fills all in all. And you He made alive, who were dead in trespasses and sins, in which you once walked according to the course of this world, according to the prince of the power of the air, the spirit who now

works in the sons of disobedience, among whom also we all once conducted ourselves in the lusts of our flesh, fulfilling the desires of the flesh and of the mind, and were by nature children of wrath, just as the others. But God, who is rich in mercy, because of His great love with which He loved us, even when we were dead in trespasses, made us alive together with Christ (by grace you have been saved), and raised us up together, and made us sit together in the heavenly places in Christ Jesus, that in the ages to come He might show the exceeding riches of His grace in His kindness toward us in Christ Jesus (1:20–2:7).

How exciting! In the spirit we are united with Christ in His ascension into heaven. So when I say ascend, I mean get up, come up and be restored! Walk in His presence and light! Break open a new day! Grow! Increase! Leap forth! Rise up and worship! Isaiah 60:1 puts it this way: "Arise, shine; for your light has come! And the glory of the LORD is risen upon you."

I've counted the cost, I have stepped across the line
I can't be bought off, scared off, lured away, or compromised
Now my way is straight, and my road is narrow
I know He's watching me 'cause His eye is on the sparrow
And I'm leaning on the everlasting arm until the storm goes by
No more murmuring and no more complaining
No more excuses and no more blaming
No more fear or unbelief or mediocrity
I'm gonna get prayed up, paid up
Lord I'm gonna grow up

Whenever there's a need
You can bet I'm gonna show up
And when Jesus comes for His bride
He won't have any problem recognizing me.[3]

Notes

1. Greg Laurie, ed., *New Believer's Bible* (Wheaton, IL: Tyndale House Publishers, 1996), p. A1.
2. Paul Lee Tan, *Encyclopedia of 7,700 Illustrations* (Garland, TX: Bible Communications, Inc., 1996), n.p.
3. Chuck D. Pierce, *Let the Lion of Judah Roar*, (Denton, TX: Glory of Zion International Ministries, Inc., 2001).

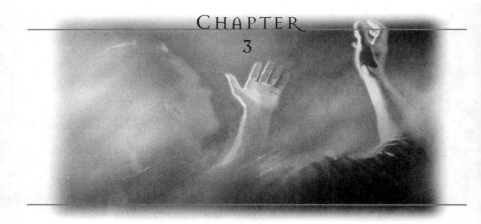

Let Us Go So That We May Worship!

When I was a child, I went with my grandmother to her country Baptist church in east Texas. The people there knew how to worship God. I would often watch with intrigue a lady in her 80s named Mrs. Grimes as she would stand up, sing and wave her hands. It was as if the God in the Bible stories was so real to her that she actually could feel His touch.

The pastor would ask, "Mrs. Grimes, what is happening with you?" She always said the same thing: "I feel His presence around me. He's speaking to me."

Watching and listening to Mrs. Grimes instilled in me a desire to also know the Lord's presence and hear His voice. Not only did I want to raise my hands when I sang in church, but also I wanted God's touch in all the contours of my life. This is what the late author and worship leader David Morris called a lifestyle of worship.[1]

A CLOSER LOOK AT LIFE

Before we can understand how to make worship our lifestyle, we need to take a closer look at life itself. The word "life" is used in the Bible to describe the animating force in both animals and humans (see Gen. 1:20; 2:7; 7:15). Our existence in a flesh-and-blood body is subject to a full array of feelings and experiences, including suffering, illness, toil, temptations and sin. However, God can show us how to worship in the midst of these resistant forces. We can live an abundant life and accomplish our God-given purpose here on Earth. To do this, worship must become a lifestyle.

> All life depends upon God for its creation and maintenance.

All life depends upon God for its creation and maintenance. It is easy enough to grasp and embrace God as our Creator (see Gen. 1). It is a bit harder to allow Him to be our sustainer. We tend to want to take control of our daily lives and our destinies. But if we are to become worship warriors, we must discover how we can keep the life cycle of God flowing within us. In *The Best Is*

Yet Ahead, Becky Sytsema and I write about the life cycle God has given us.

> God has a cycle of life for each one of us. Our life cycle begins at conception and moves along in the following progression:
>
> 1. Conception is the beginning of God's purpose by knitting us together in the womb.
> 2. Birth is the bringing forth of the new life God has created.
> 3. Age of accountability with an awareness of our need for God.
> 4. Rebirth when we are quickened from darkness into light.
> 5. Receiving hope by searching for and receiving the expectation of God for our future.
> 6. Maturing of our faith into an overcoming weapon of God.
> 7. Demonstration of God's power and wisdom that unlocks our destiny.
> 8. Manifestation of God's glory and inner fulfillment of our identity in Him.
> 9. A completion of our role in the earth realm, facing death and entering into eternity.
>
> The enemy loves to interrupt the life cycle in any one of these stages so that the fulfillment of our destiny cannot be completed. He would love for us to miss the *kairos* or opportune time that the Lord has in each of the phases above. If you miss that *now* time, it does not mean that things will never be back in order, it just means you postpone what God wants to do, and you enter into a prolonged wilderness season.

We all have wilderness seasons that are ordained of God where we are moving from one season to another. However, we can prolong this wilderness season. Jesus stayed in His wilderness season for 40 days, whereas the Israelites stayed in their wilderness season for 40 years. The Israelites were held captive in their wilderness season because of their unbelief and hardness of heart, whereas Jesus resisted the devil in His wilderness season and came out filled with power for His future. The choice is ours![2]

I believe that our decisions regarding worship affect each phase of our life cycles. If we choose not to worship in one phase, then we distance ourselves from God and prolong our wilderness experience.

In the book *God's Timing for Your Life*, Dutch Sheets writes, "Life is a series of changes—a process of going from the old to the new—from *chronos* [a general process of time] to *kairos* [an opportune, strategic or *now* time]. Growth, change, revival—all are processes. Life is connected. Not understanding this, we tend to despise the *chronos* times of preparing, sowing, believing and persevering. . . . We're not losing or wasting time, we're investing it. And if we do so faithfully, the shift *will* come."[3]

God creates by giving His breath or Spirit to creatures. Life can only be given by God, and only God can sustain life. If we stop seeking God our life in Him will stall. We will get lost in our pursuit of His will on Earth. What is living has movement. By contrast, in death all movement ceases. So we must keep moving in the Lord.

THE WAY TO DEVELOP A LIFESTYLE OF WORSHIP

The Old Testament uses bold metaphors for fellowship with God. Consider what the psalmist penned: "For with You is the fountain of life: in Your light we see light" (Ps. 36:9). Another psalmist pleaded for God's hand to be upon him: "Then we will not turn back from You; revive us, and we will call upon Your name" (Ps. 80:18).

The proper response to life as the gift from God is to live every day in service to God (see Isa. 38:10-20), obey the Law (see Lev. 18:5), do God's will (see Matt. 6:10; 7:21) and feed upon God's Word (see Deut. 6:1-9; 8:3; 32:46-47; Matt. 4:4). Only when a life is lived in obedience to God does it deserve to be called life (see Deut. 30:15-20; Ezek. 3:16-21; 18:1-32).

The New Testament deepens this emphasis. Paul points out

Not one of us lives for himself, and not one dies for himself; for if we live, we live for the Lord, or if we die, we die for the Lord; therefore whether we live or die, we are the Lord's. For to this end Christ died and lived again, that He might be Lord both of the dead and of the living (Rom. 14:7-9, *NASB*).

Such a life demands fellowship with the Savior who, after all, is the purpose of life.

A TIME TO SEEK AND CALL UPON THE LORD

The act of seeking is part of worship. I explained in Chapter 2 how we began to "call upon the name of the Lord." However, we must move beyond calling and become seekers of God.

Second Chronicles 7:14 declares, "If My people who are called by My name will humble themselves, and pray and seek My face, and turn from their wicked ways, then I will hear from heaven, and will forgive their sin and heal their land."

The word "seek" means to search, try to discover, request, look for or aim at.[4] It actually implies that we desire to know something or someone, and we do not stop seeking it until we connect properly with that person or revelation. How do we *seek* God's face? We are to use every dimension of prayer and worship that we know. In the context of 2 Chronicles 7:14, which is the most used and quoted prayer passage in the Bible, we find that if we will humble ourselves and seek His face, He will hear, forgive and heal us.

Jesus said, "Keep on asking and it will be given you; keep on seeking and you will find; keep on knocking [reverently] and [the door] will be opened" (Matt. 7:7, *AMP*). In this Scripture, the Lord teaches us not to hesitate to request what we need from someone in a higher position. In the original Greek usage, this is like a child requesting something from a parent or a beggar wanting sustenance from a passerby.

> ## Since God is looking for us, if we seek Him, we will surely find Him.

When we ask, we are not to command, but we are to be persistent and bold. We must strain every nerve to find God and receive from Him. In this context it is good to remember that God tells us not to worry about what we will wear, what we will eat or what we will drink in the days ahead. He said these are the things that the Gentiles seek after, but like the sparrow He will take care of those who worship Him (see Matt. 6:28-34).

God also seeks His people. "For the eyes of the LORD run to and fro throughout the whole earth, to show Himself strong on behalf of those whose heart is loyal to Him" (2 Chron. 16:9). Since God is looking for us, if we seek Him, we will surely find Him. Then the best that He has for us will be had. This will transform our lives.

WORSHIP AND TRANSFORMATION

The story of Jesus and the Samaritan woman at the well is familiar to us (see John 4). He requested a drink to satisfy His temporal thirst, but offered her everlasting water. As they stood at the well, He told her everything about herself and revealed to her great insights about worship.

Jesus told the woman that it did not matter where she worshiped; rather, it mattered that she had the right attitude and heart. He then explained that worship happens when a seeker comes into harmony with the nature and character of God and embraces His transforming Spirit. He said worship must be transparent, sincere and follow biblical mandates. He summed it up beautifully: "God is Spirit, and those who worship Him must worship in spirit and truth" (John 4:24).

When we worship God in spirit and in truth, we come face-to-face with our destinies. We move from obsession to reality. This is the transformation that took place in the Samaritan woman's life. The Lord shifted her desire, which had been aimed toward every man in the city, to Himself, and then to seeing her whole city changed. That is what worship can do. Individual worship brings transformation. But when we worship individually, we can see the territory where we live transformed as well.

When we worship, we actually break out of conformity and move into transformation. Paul wrote, "Be transformed by the renewing of your mind" (Rom. 12:2). To "transform" means to change or transfigure. This comes from the Greek word *meta-morphoo*, from which we get the word "metamorphosis." The dictionary defines "transform" as changing "the outward form or appearance of.... to change in character or condition: convert."[5] In the broadest sense, transformation is the change of external form and inner nature. I believe the only way we can do this is through worship. It draws us out of the pattern of the world into the life structure that God made for us when He knit us together in our mother's wombs.

CONTROL OF OUR APPETITES

In our harried lives, we often hit the fast-food drive-through window instead of sitting down to a well-balanced meal. We gobble up Big Macs, macho burritos and Twinkies. The easy feast satisfies our hunger and saves time, so we go back again and again, virtually neglecting our nutritional needs.

Many of us approach worship in the same way. We go about filling our God-shaped voids the same way we fill our stomachs. We put a Bible verse on the refrigerator, a bumper sticker on our car and a highlight mark on our favorite verse in Psalms. We consider our meager efforts worship, then wonder why we still experience an emptiness in our souls. Not seeing our need for true worship, we continue to generate the fast-food equivalents. Eventually, due to starvation, our bodies respond in the wrong way.

John Dickson provides this insight:

I always used to hang around when my mom cooked her desserts. I wanted to lick the bowl or eat the leftover cookie dough. I always wanted more than was in the bowl. One day she let me have all the dough I wanted. My stomach got filled, but strangely. My stomach then began to ache. What I thought would bring me the utmost satisfaction had instead left me languishing in misery. I was full but not satisfied. I never did that again. Many times this is what happens to us spiritually. Our bodies do not want cookie dough; rather, they want nutritious food. Proper nutrition gives us energy. We feel good about ourselves, and we have a feeling of satisfaction that we are eating correctly.

Jesus is quoted in John 6:35-44, "I AM the bread of life: he that cometh to me shall never hunger; and he that believeth on me shall never thirst" (*KJV*, emphasis added).

We must eat daily the True Bread. And we must eat ample amounts, so we do not end up getting hungry and grabbing on to a substitute, such as a Twinkie, halfway through the afternoon. One little bite will not fill us up. When I sit down to a meal, it takes more than one bean to satisfy me. One bean will not give me the strength and energy I need to get through my day. A few weeks of having one little bean a day would leave me much thinner than I am now. Losing weight might be a blessing, but I would also be much weaker. This is also true with spiritual vitality. We grab one little bite of the Bread of Life and wonder why we are spiritually emaciated and weak. However, a true seeker is filled. Once we are filled and satisfied by Jesus, we become spiritual food and refreshment to others. Allow the Lord to overflow you with the fullness of His Spirit-filled life. Not only will He satisfy you, but also He will satisfy those around you.

WEIGHTS THAT KEEP US FROM ASCENDING

Only by the Spirit of God can we ascend. Think of the analogy of a hot-air balloon. When the fire heats the air within the balloon and causes it to fill, this allows the balloon to become buoyant. As a matter of fact, there need to be guy wires to hold the balloon down.

> ## Once the Spirit of God starts filling us, Satan tries anything he can to keep us from ascending.

I believe Satan works the same way. Once the Spirit of God starts filling us, he tries anything he can to keep us from ascending into our position in heaven. He hooks and grabs hold of our spirits and tries to keep us out of the authority of our position in Christ. He knows that if we ever get fully in that abiding place, we will do him in.

As we seek the Lord and move into a posture of worship, our souls and spirits are divided. This is how we are cut loose to ascend. Hebrews 4:12 declares:

> For the Word that God speaks is alive and full of power [making it active, operative, energizing, and effective]; it is sharper than any two-edged sword, penetrating to the dividing line of the breath of life (soul) and [the immortal] spirit, and of joints and marrow [of the deepest parts of our nature], exposing and sifting and analyzing and judging the very thoughts and purposes of the heart (*AMP*).

Once this division occurs, personal warfare becomes a reality. As we ascend in worship, we also begin to see more clearly the war of resistance over God's redemptive plan. Some people call this the filling of the Spirit. Others call it the baptism of the Spirit. Whatever we call it, this is the reality: We are filled with His Spirit so we can continue to accomplish His goal on Earth. First John 3:8 explains it this way:

> [But] he who commits sin [who practices evildoing] is of the devil [takes his character from the evil one], for the devil has sinned (violated the divine law) from the beginning. The reason the Son of God was made manifest (visible) was to undo (destroy, loosen, and dissolve) the works the devil [has done] (*AMP*).

We are influenced by the Holy Spirit rather than evil spirits that in the past have gained access to our human natures.

Our spirits get to know perfect freedom. This part of who we are should remain light and floating, like a hot air balloon. This is how we continue to grow and know joy and how we are empowered to do the work of the Lord in the earthly realm. If we ascend in worship, then when Satan attempts to steal these elements of spiritual life from us, we can recognize the loss. Without a disciplined life of worship, we cannot recognize oppression or weight that begins to hold our spirits from ascending into the position that God has given us in the heavens (see Eph. 1—2).

THE PATTERN OF MOSES

In the Bible, the greater the bondage, the louder the cry of God's people for God to intervene on their behalf. This cry caused God to hear their groaning and remember His covenant with their forefathers. Exodus 2:25 reads, "And God looked upon the children of Israel, and God acknowledged them." Then the angel of the Lord appeared to Moses and commissioned him to deliver

God's people, so they could go and worship Him in the way He had ordained for them to worship.

What was established with Moses will become a latter-day pattern, not only for modern-day Israel but also for worship. We find strong parallels in the book of Revelation concerning worship in the latter days. Dan Juster, in his book *Revelation: The Passover Key*, writes the following:

> The world parallels the Egypt of Exodus. The people of God are represented by the Israelites in Egypt. As Israel was protected in Goshen, so God will mark believers and protect them from the plagues. Unlike the Israelites, the believers will be protected in various places throughout the world. The sons of Israel overcame the angel of death because the blood of the lamb was upon their doorposts. Believers in the last days will overcome Satan by the blood of the Lamb (Jesus), by the word of their testimony and by not loving their own lives unto death. The Antichrist of the last days is paralleled by the Pharaoh. Furthermore, the last days people of God will have an extraordinary escape, as did the Israelites in their escape through the sea. This time, the believers are taken through the veil between the seen and unseen world into Heaven and return with the Messiah. As the Egyptians foolishly pursued Israel, so the armies of the Antimessiah will foolishly pursue Israel by sending his armies into her land to oppose the nation of the Jews and the armies of Heaven returning with the Messiah. As Pharaoh's troops were supernaturally defeated in the sea, so the armies of the Antichrist will be supernaturally defeated in a great conflagration (see Rev. 19; Zech. 14).[6]

Remember, worship was the true issue. Moses would confront Pharaoh and say, "Let My people go that they might worship Me." There would be a plague and a confrontation. However, Pharaoh, a satanic figure-type, would harden his heart and say, "I do not want to let you go." Another plague would come. Finally, Pharaoh was willing to let a portion of the people go, but not all of them (see Exod. 5). Similarly, there is a progression that we go through to come into an established place of worship. The enemy will hold on to anything he can within us—individually, corporately or territorially—to keep us from coming into that place of worship that releases covenant blessings.

A New Form of Worship

With the final plague God shifted how His people would worship Him. This is not some idiosyncratic notion; rather, it is clear that the Passover, which points toward the ultimate Lamb of God, who is Jesus, instituted a new form of worship. If the Jewish people were to be protected in the midst of this plague

> The blood of Jesus is the initial element that we must embrace if we are to come into true worship.

that would eventually kill the firstborn of Egypt, they had to place blood on their doorposts. Similarly, the blood of the Lord Jesus Christ is the initial element that we must embrace if we are to come into true worship, which includes sacrifice. God was leading the Jewish people out to worship Him, yet worship never really took hold in this first-generation's hearts. We must have a determination to cut ties with every iniquitous pattern in our bloodlines, so we can come into a full place of worship, service and sacrifice before the Lord.

The Lord understood that the Jewish people were not adequately established in worship. Therefore, He did not want them to go out by the way of the land of the Philistines "lest perhaps the people change their minds when they see war, and return to Egypt" (Exod. 13:17). God knew He would have to establish a worship pattern in them before they were confronted with other enemies; otherwise they would retreat into an old pattern and their former lifestyle. I cover this more in a later chapter.

THE MAGNIFICATION OF THE LORD

The Bible instructs us to magnify the Lord. Psalm 34:1-3 reads, "I will bless the LORD at all times; His praise shall continually be in my mouth. My soul shall make its boast in the LORD; the humble shall hear of it and be glad. Oh, magnify the LORD with me, and let us exalt His name together." Why? It happens because the devil's earthly advertising program has made God small in our eyes. We must make Him large! Magnify Him. How do we do this? One way is to praise Him.

When we feed upon the true Bread of Life, we begin to fill the God-shaped void with God Himself. As this happens, we satisfy the natural desire within us to worship. Paul wrote, "I discipline my body and bring it into subjection" (1 Cor. 9:27). John Dickson admits that he has to tell himself to put down that Twinkie. When he obeys, he begins to taste and see that the Lord is good. Isaiah 55:1-2 reads,

Ho! Everyone who thirsts, come to the waters; and you who have no money, come, buy and eat. Yes, come, buy wine and milk without money and without price. Why do you spend money for what is not bread, and your wages for what does not satisfy? Listen carefully to Me, and eat what is good, and let your soul delight itself in abundance.

God has prepared a table before us in the presence of our enemies (see Ps. 23:5). His Spirit says, "Come." Let us eat. Let us meditate. Let us exercise that which we are obtaining from Him. Let us work out our salvation. Let us praise. Let us worship.

Mary: An Example to Follow

The best biblical example of magnifying the Lord in worship and making Him big come from Mary's example, which is recorded in Luke 1. The angel of the Lord visits Mary and gives her favor. He announces that she will be overshadowed by the Holy Spirit. This overshadowing is a visitation of God's glory upon her, very much like a cloud surrounding her.

The angel tells Mary that she will be the carrier of the Son of God. He then tells her that with God nothing will be impossible. Mary must bypass her own understanding to accept this. She comes into full agreement with the word, and says, "Behold the maidservant of the Lord! Let it be to me according to your word" (Luke 1:38).

The angel also announces that Mary's relative Elizabeth would conceive a son. This birth would happen first. When Mary visits Elizabeth, who was much older, and sees that Elizabeth has actually conceived a child, faith begins to move in the earthly realm. Both Mary and Elizabeth are filled with faith.

Mary then begins to sing a song of magnification. This song has been known through the ages as the "Magnificat." It is a tremendous example for us as to how we should operate in magnifying the Lord when He puts something in our hearts that is too big for us. Here is Mary's song:

My soul magnifies the Lord, and my spirit has rejoiced in God my Savior. For He has regarded the lowly state of His maidservant; for behold, henceforth all generations will call me blessed. For He who is mighty has done great things for me, and holy is His name (Luke 1:46-49).

THE DISCIPLINE OF WORSHIP

Part of our discipline in the Lord comes when we worship Him despite our circumstances. Hebrews 12:5-6 reads, "My son, do not regard lightly the discipline of the Lord, nor faint when you are reproved by Him; for those whom the Lord loves He disciplines, and He scourges every son whom He receives" (*NASB*). The word "discipline" used in this verse means more than just to punish for disobedience. The Greek is *paideuo*, which means to train up a child and to educate him as well as to discipline him with appropriate punishment when there is disobedience. This passage in Hebrews quotes from Proverbs 3:11-13, "My son, do not reject the discipline of the LORD, or loathe His reproof, for whom the LORD loves He reproves, even as a father corrects the son in whom he delights" (*NASB*).

John Dickson says:

Here the Hebrew word for discipline, *muwcar*, means warning, instruction; also restraint. The Lord was training me up as a worshiper, educating, warning, instructing and restraining me as well as chastening me as a father would correct a son in whom he delights. Sometimes I would ask, "God, what did I do wrong? Just let me know and I'll repent." But it wasn't always a matter of what I had done wrong, it was a matter of what the Lord was building in me. I have heard it said, there is glory on the mountaintop, but the fruit grows in the valley. Our praise cannot be limited to our mountaintop experiences. It must be tested in the valley.

You don't have to be in full-time ministry to live a lifestyle of worship. You just have to direct that natural propensity for worship in the right direction—toward God. He wants to be a part of our daily lives, not just our Sunday mornings.

Can we only worship in a climate-controlled building, in a soft seat, led by skilled musicians and singing well-crafted songs? Early in our Christian lives, my wife, Violet, and I were in a stagnant church, but every Friday night a charismatic Episcopal church in Dallas, the Church of the Resurrection, had a special praise service. We would "truck up" and refresh our souls. One Friday night, we had made the 50-mile trip. Violet was delivering our young son, Michael, to the nursery, and I was finding a good seat. The church had a lot of glass and the afternoon sun was glaring through, right where I had picked a seat. It was very annoying, but it was a good seat, and I knew the sun would be going down soon and the music would start and I would be lost in praise. Just then, the Lord spoke to my heart, "Praise Me."

"Yes, Lord, as soon as that sun goes down and the music starts, I am going to lose myself in praise to You."

"Praise Me now," came the reply.

"Now, with no music, and the sun shining in my eyes?"

"Yes, now."

I stood up, raised my hands and, before the worship team had a chance to lead me, I opened my heart and offered to God a sacrifice of praise. I worshiped and adored Him. The love of the Father flooded down on me.

It was the best time of worship I had ever had in that church. No longer was I dependent on a worship leader to lead me.

A DETERMINATION TO PRAISE HIM

John Dickson has a lot of great stories and insights. Here is another:

> For several years I owned and operated a Christian bookstore. This was a wonderful experience, but there was a time when the store went through a financial crisis. I thought it was going to go under. It was a time of great stress and anxiety. A feeling of dread burned in the pit of my stomach, but the Lord instructed me to go to the store two hours before it opened each day and walk around inside and lift my hands and praise Him. My heart was like wax within me, my hands felt like lead weights, my mouth was like sawdust. Fear and dread were in my thoughts, not praise. But I knew what I needed to do. Job had testified, "Though He slay me, yet will I trust Him" (Job 13:15). I began to walk around, praising at the top of my lungs. Like David, I said, "Bless the LORD, O my soul; and all that is within me, bless His holy name" (Ps. 103:1). Sometimes we just have to tell our soul what to do. Our soul does not always feel like praising Him. As I praised Him as an act of my will, my spirit began to awaken inside me. As my soul began to line up with my proclamations, a flow of anointing began to be released. The oppressive cloud would lift, and the presence of God would come into my store. Over time the business turned around, and I knew it was not because of my keen business

acumen. I am a worship leader. I can barely balance my checkbook. I could write three songs in the time it takes me to struggle through my bank statement. It was the Lord. He turned my circumstances around because I praised Him in the hard place.

So what I do as a worship leader was not learned on

It was the Lord. He turned my circumstances around because I praised Him in the hard place.

---

the stage, but in daily life. That is where our worship should be the strongest and the most vibrant. It is not our musical training that qualifies us as worshipers, but our sold-out hearts for God. Matt Redman writes:

> The heart of God loves a persevering worshipper, who though overwhelmed by many troubles, is overwhelmed even more by the beauty of God.[7]

When Paul and Silas were beaten and thrown in jail, they were found praising (see Acts 16:25). Jonah praised from the belly of a whale (see Jon. 2). When they were flogged, Peter and the apostles rejoiced that they had been considered worthy to suffer shame for Jesus' name (see Acts 5:40-41). Peter later wrote,

> In this [our salvation] you greatly rejoice, even though now for a little while, if necessary, you

have been distressed by various trials, that the proof of your faith, being more precious than gold which is perishable, even though tested by fire, may be found to result in praise and glory and honor at the revelation of Jesus Christ (1 Pet. 1:6-7, *NASB*).

When things are wonderful, we praise Him. When things are horrible, we praise Him. Whether we are happy or sad or terrified or bored, we are determined to offer to God our sacrifice of praise. Everything in us should give praise to the Lord.

A WAY TO PRAISE HIM ALL DAY

But you are a chosen generation, a royal priesthood, a holy nation, His own special people, that you may proclaim the praises of Him who called you out of darkness into His marvelous light (1 Pet. 2:9).

Paul exhorts us to rejoice in the Lord *always!* (see Phil. 4:4). King David said, "His praise shall *continually* be in my mouth" (Ps. 34:1, emphasis added). Asaph declared, "My praise shall be *continually* of You" (Ps. 71:6, emphasis added). Psalm 119:164 reads, "Seven times a day I praise You."

If we take the last psalmist literally, that means we are to praise God every few hours. We could set the alarm on our wristwatch to alert us. Buzzzzz—9 A.M., "Lord, I haven't praised You since I got up this morning. Let me just tell You how much You mean to me. I love You, Lord." Buzzzzz—11 A.M., "Lord, I'm late for my meeting. You are my strength and my salvation. I know You can help me through. I praise You with all my heart. You are my ever-present help in times of need." If we did this our day would take on a different perspective. We might even find ourselves praising Him in the midst of difficulties. Buzzzz—5 P.M., "Lord, I forgot my anniversary! Lord, thank You for Your great grace. Pour Your grace out on my wife right now, Lord, before I get home. You are a good God." Buzzzz—11 P.M. "Lord, thank You so much for getting me through this day. I love You and"— zzzzzzz.

THE PROCESSION BEGINS

Some people only want to worship, and others only want to be warriors. Both praise and war are necessary. War should come out of worship.

In Song of Solomon, we find a key principle. The Old Testament book presents a passionate exchange between a man and a woman with love as its central theme. The Song celebrates the potential of love when expressed in the covenant of marriage. This mirrors the relationship between God and man.

Song of Solomon reads:

> Who is this coming out of the wilderness like pillars of smoke, perfumed with myrrh and frankincense, with all the merchant's fragrant powders? Behold, it is Solomon's couch, with sixty valiant men around it, of the valiant of Israel. They all hold swords, being expert in war. Every man has his sword on his thigh because of fear in the night. Of the wood of Lebanon Solomon the King made himself a palanquin (3:6-9).

The palanquin, or royal wedding bed, coming out of the wilderness to Zion is a picture of the redemptive journey of the Ark of the Covenant. This is the same journey that each of us must make in worship. Who is coming out of the wilderness? is a good question for each one of us to ask ourselves. We could put it this way: Are we going to keep following the pillar of fire and the cloud, or are we going to enter the Promised Land?

This concept connects worship with warriors. It implies that those who worship and carry forth the Ark will have swords and be experts in warfare. Therefore, when we worship, God's presence surrounds us. His presence also equips us for war.

Notes

1. David Morris, *A Lifestyle of Worship* (Ventura, CA: Renew, 1998), n.p.
2. Chuck D. Pierce and Rebecca Wagner Sytsema, *The Best Is Yet Ahead* (Colorado Springs, CO: Wagner Publications, 2001), pp. 27-28.
3. Dutch Sheets, *God's Timing for Your Life* (Ventura, CA: Regal Books, 2001), pp. 17-18.
4. *Merriam-Webster's Collegiate Dictionary*, 10th ed., s.v. "seek."
5. Ibid., s.v. "transform."
6. Dan Juster, *Revelation: The Passover Key* (Shippensburg, PA: Destiny Image Publishers, 1991), p. 19.
7. Matt Redman, *The Unquenchable Worshipper*, (Ventura, CA: Regal Books, 2001), n.p.

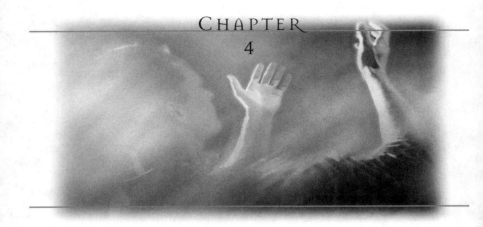

JESUS
ASCENDED

Arise to Your Throne, Lion of Judah
Make Your Glory known throughout the land
As our praises ascend
May Your Kingdom without end
Be established in all the earth
CHUCK D. PIERCE, *LET THE LION OF JUDAH ROAR*

Jesus was the ultimate worshiper. His example of seeking the Father should be the example each of us should follow.

At a wedding, He changed water into wine. This began God's glory moving on Earth in a way that humankind had never known. His glory was manifested everywhere He went. He healed people. He broke the power of death by raising some from the dead. He taught a new form and method of worship. He gathered disciples and taught them how to seek the Father. He sidestepped the enemy, thus staying on the Father's perfect timetable. He faced His enemies with confidence, revelation and quietness. He raised one of His dearest friends from the grave and removed grave clothes from him. This intensified animosity along His path. However, Luke 9:51 reads, "Now it came to pass, when the time had come for Him to be [revealed] that He steadfastly set His face to go to Jerusalem."

When Jesus entered Jerusalem, He displayed great emotion. He wept over the city, knowing He would be rejected by His people. His procession and worship of the Father led Him to the Cross. The mocking worship that took place at the foot of the Cross did not keep Him from hanging obediently before the Father. At this point, He gave up His Spirit and surrendered fully back to the Father. From the Cross, He was taken to the tomb. However, because He had been obedient and fully submissive, the tomb could not hold Him. Father God fully empowered Him to overcome death, descend to hell and then ascend to be seated next to the Father in the Throne Room. What an example of worship and proceeding forth!

JESUS AND ASCENSION

For the purpose of this book, I write of two ascensions of Jesus. The first ascension is what He did through prayer and intimate communion with the Father. This is an experience we as humans can also have. All biblical prayer and communion is a type of ascension to the Throne Room and presence of God.

Of course, Jesus is the example *par excellence* of communion, fellowship and prayer. The Lord's Prayer is a pattern He gave the disciples to follow to teach them to have similar intimacy and fellowship with the Father.

The second ascension is Jesus' historical ascension to heaven, which is recorded in Acts 1. There, we learn that Jesus is received into a cloud and returns to the Father. The New Testament declares that Jesus ascended to and sat down at the right hand of the Father (see Heb. 1:1-3). From heaven Christ currently reigns, and from heaven He will come again to judge the living and the dead.

It is on the basis of this second ascension that Ephesians 4:7-12 shows us:

> But to each one of us grace was given according to the measure of Christ's gift. Therefore He says: "When He ascended on high, He led captivity captive, and gave gifts to men." (Now this, "He ascended"—what does it mean but that He also first descended into the lower parts of the earth? He who descended is also the One who ascended far above all the heavens, that He might fill all things.) And He Himself gave some to be apostles, some prophets, some evangelists, and some pastors and teachers, for the equipping of the saints for the work of ministry, for the edifying of the body of Christ.

A wonderful prayer by Paul is recorded in Ephesians 1:15. The apostle declares that the God of our Lord Jesus Christ, the Father of glory, would give us the spirit of wisdom and revelation in the knowledge of Him. He then prayed that the eyes of our understanding would be enlightened, that we would know the hope of His calling for our lives. He went on to share that Jesus had put all things under His feet and that He had been given to the Church to be head over all things. He then began to share with the church in Ephesus that even though they had walked in darkness and disobedience, aligned with the prince of the power of the air, God, through His rich mercy and grace, had extended and made His love available so that they could be made alive with Christ. Oh, what a marvelous grace! This aliveness causes us to be raised up together and seated with Christ Jesus in heavenly places. We are in union with Him in His resurrection, in His ascension and in His rulership. This union allows us to share in the present works of His kingdom power.

> **B**ecause Jesus has paved the way for us, He has given us the right to ascend.

Because Jesus has paved the way and become the model for us, He has given us the right to ascend and then gives us even greater access to the Father's Throne Room than Old Testament believers had. When He ascended, He gave gifts to mankind. Most of us know these gifts as the fivefold ministry gifts. I call them the ascension gifts that govern Earth. Jesus released these gifts back down to individuals on Earth so that we would maintain the strata. Without us ascending, we can never come into the fullness of the unity of these gifts or exercise the faith that overcomes the evil workings of the enemy within Earth.

OPERATION OF THE GIFTS TODAY

Jesus gave the gifts on His way up with the directive that they would mature through the ages until we come to the unity of the faith and of the knowledge of the Son of God. Without these gifts in operation, we can never reach this goal. Through the generations these gifts were not mature and the Church did not worship in fullness. As a result, the Body of Christ was tossed about with every wind of doctrine and trickery of man.

Cunning craftiness of deceitful plotting in certain generations attempted to overthrow the power of God working on Earth through the Church. When we do not worship and intercede and allow these gifts to come to their next level of maturity in every generation, God's influence over the Church in the world is less than it should be. Therefore, for total restoration to occur in the earthly realm and be maintained, these gifts must be operational.

The desire of Jesus was for the gifts to mature from generation to generation until He returns for His Bride. The only way we can become without spot or wrinkle is through this maturation process.

This is a time for worship! This is a time for intercessors to ascend, worship and come boldly into our Father's Throne Room. We must cry out for the craftiness on Earth to be stopped!

This is a time to petition our Father for His gifts to be manifested in all nations on Earth! This is a time for prophets to grab hold of the revelation that is being petitioned and declared so that the gifts will come into full operation. This is the time for those who are operating in these gifts to worship in a new way, to gain God's strategies and to move in His authority.

THE EFFECT OF JESUS' ASCENSION ON EARTH

Let's think about this for a moment. While the people watched, Jesus ASCENDED! He had promised His ascension during the time He trained His disciples, before His crucifixion. Now His followers were watching Him fulfill His promise.

It is difficult for us to grasp the concept of ascension. Yet if we press further, we find that Jesus' ascension also provide promises and hope for us for the future. Jesus instructed His disciples on the concept. He began teaching them, as recorded in John 3, about the new birth—a form of ascension. He then showed them that upon repentance a new order of life opens up to the believer. This new order comes with an abundance of blessings and a personal relationship with God. The new believer will begin to see the kingdom of God around and in him or her. Faith comes to life. The new believer actually enters into a new realm. This is how we experience the promises of God becoming realities in our lives, including access to the Throne Room. This, however, is not an easy concept to understand. It is probably easier to ascend and enter into a new dimension of spiritual life than it is to understand it. I write more on entering the Throne Room in following chapters.

THE RELATIONSHIP BETWEEN SALVATION AND ASCENSION

Jesus told Nicodemus, who was a ruler and a Pharisee, about a new birth experience that must come "from above" (see John 3). That is what the "again" in "born-again" means. In other words, something spiritual would have to happen in order for his eyes to be opened, and it would have to come by the Spirit.

The Lord asked Nicodemus how he could teach Israel if he had not witnessed what he was teaching. Then Jesus makes an interesting statement: "If I have told you earthly things and you do not believe, how will you believe if I tell you heavenly things? No one has ascended to heaven but He who came down from heaven, that is, the Son of Man who is in heaven" (John 3:12-13). This means that our salvation experience begins with an understanding of ascension, being born "from above."

Jesus goes on to say, "For God so loved the world that He gave His only begotten Son, that whoever believes in Him should not perish but have everlasting life" (John 3:16).

The concept of ascending opens eternity to us. Jesus could have said something like this:

> If you will love and follow me, be born "from above," you will experience the love that I have for you. I have chosen to love you. I have an unconquerable, undefeatable benevolence that I want to extend toward you. I will never have any thoughts toward you except the highest good. I am motivated to give you love. I can redeem you from the grasp of the world, and that one which controls the world. Worship me! Ascend! And experience this love that I have sacrificially offered you.

PROMISES THAT RELATE TO ASCENSION

There are many promises and benefits related to ascension. For example, Jesus told His disciples:

> "Let not your heart be troubled; you believe in God, believe also in Me. In My Father's house are many mansions; if it were not so, I would have told you. I go to prepare a place for you. And if I go and prepare a place for you, I will come again and receive you to Myself; that where I am, there you may be also. And where I go you know, and the way you know." Thomas said to Him, "Lord, we do not know where You are going, and how can we know the way?" Jesus said to him, "I am the way, the truth, and the life. No one comes to the Father except through Me" (John 14:1-6).

If no one can come to the Father except through Jesus, and Jesus is teaching in these incredibly comforting Scriptures the principle of ascension, then it is probably wise to learn it.

> These are among the most comforting words in all of Scripture; from Jesus' own lips, we receive the promise of His return. He spoke these words during His most intimate time with His disciples, and they echo down to us as a precious promise to the bride of Christ. In this text Jesus tells us of a peace, a place, and a promise. He begins with a comforting exhortation: do not be troubled; be at peace. Our peace is based on our belief in God and Christ. We know that He is trustworthy and that give us a foundation of peace upon which to build our lives. Second, Jesus spoke of a place. He has promised to prepare for us a place where we will have eternal fellowship with Him. Finally, we have His personal promise that He is returning for us. Think of it! His personal signature is on our salvation; as we have received Him, He is coming to receive us. We look forward to that day in expectation, preparing ourselves for it, for "everyone who has this hope . . . purifies himself" (1 John 3:3).[1]

PRINCIPLES OF ASCENSION

Here are some biblical promises that come with ascension. When we ascend in worship, we can expect to experience these things.

1. We have an assurance that a heavenly place has been prepared for us (see John 14:1-2).
2. There is power in the supernatural connection, and we have access to the Father and all of His love (see John 14:5-7).
3. We will receive revelation of who the Father is (see John 14:21).

4. Jesus ascended so the Helper (the Holy Spirit) could come to Earth on our behalf. Therefore, if we worship and ascend, we are promised that the Holy Spirit will fill our lives. He will bring conviction when we sin, open the way for us to experience our righteousness through faith and condemn the devil on our behalf (see John 16:7-9).

5. We will be comforted during our suffering (see Acts 7:54-60).

6. Because He ascended, He can reveal heaven's call (see Acts 9:1-18).

7. We can see the new doors that open for ministry on Earth (see 1 Cor. 16:9).

8. We can be released in and aligned with the gifts that will allow us to demonstrate God's power, authority and rule in the earthly realm (see Eph. 4:7-12).

9. We can demonstrate the life-changing power of the gospel (see Col. 3:1-4).

10. We can experience the Lord standing with us and strengthening us so that we might accomplish His will on Earth. We can experience the power of His ascension and deliverance from every evil work (see 2 Tim. 4:16-18).

11. From His ascension, He demonstrated that glory, not death, is the final word of operation in our lives (see Heb. 2:9).

12. From ascension, we can always have a final victory (see Rev. 1:1).

FOLLOW JESUS IN ASCENSION

Jesus calls us forth and says, "Follow me" (see John 1:43). I love the passages in John 1 that record how He selected His disciples.

He called Andrew and Peter. He then found Philip. Then the Word of God notes that Philip found Nathanael. Philip started to bring Nathanael to Jesus. John 1:47-49 recounts the story:

> Jesus saw Nathanael coming toward Him, and said of him, "Behold, an Israelite indeed, in whom is no deceit!" Nathanael said to Him, "How do You know me?" Jesus answered and said to him, "Before Philip called you, when you were under the fig tree, I saw you." Nathanael answered and said to Him, "Rabbi, You are the Son of God! You are the King of Israel!"

I love how worship and ascension work together. Once we go up to the Throne Room and gain revelation from the Father, we descend (again, this is spiritual movement not a physical one) and begin to share it down here on Earth.

Jesus calls us forth and says, "Follow me."

I appreciate Nathanael's skeptical attitude. I have found through my three decades of walking with the Lord that I run into questions and hesitations all the time. I love to seek God then share with others what He has shown to me. But many people, because they have not gone up into the Throne Room through worship themselves, have a difficult time comprehending the revelation. This is how Nathanael responded to Philip. But then, when Nathanael came to Jesus along with Philip, Jesus changed Nathanael's whole outlook. Jesus released supernatural insight into Nathanael's character. Nathanael knew that he had been confronted by the Son of God.

Jesus had just the right words: "Before Philip called you, when you were under the fig tree, I saw you" (v. 48). Because Jesus sits at the right hand of the Father, He has an awesome view. He knows everything about us. When we ascend to our position in the heavens, He begins to reveal information and insight. He shows us why we were created and what God wants us to do. Once Nathanael acknowledged that Jesus had a heavenly perspective, Jesus was able to reveal to him principles about faith, ascension, revelation and heavenly perspective.

A HEAVENLY PORTAL OPENS

Jesus answered and said to him, "Because I said to you, 'I saw you under the fig tree,' do you believe? You will see greater things than these." And He said to him, "Most assuredly, I say to you, hereafter you shall see heaven open, and the angels of God ascending and descending upon the Son of Man" (John 1:50-51).

Once we recognize who Jesus is, the heavens open up to us. This is what Jesus was saying to Nathanael: "Now that you have recognized me, you have access to revelation you have never had before."

A similar experience occurred in Jacob's life. Genesis 25—28 relates the story. Isaac spoke a powerful blessing over Jacob that would transcend through the generations. However, this blessing bypassed the normal earthly order of the firstborn.

Isaac's wife, Rebekah, had seen the weakness of character in her firstborn son, Esau, and therefore positioned her favorite son, Jacob, to be the recipient of the blessing. She attempted to convince, rearrange and manipulate events.

In her plan, the blessing would pass on through Jacob to the generations to come. How would this work? How does the blessing of God get connected and passed on from generation to generation? The answer is related to the principle of ascending and descending in worship.

> Our mistakes do not stop
> the chain forming that is linked to
> the divine purpose of God.

For Jacob to experience the fullness of this blessing, he was sent away to find a wife that would be aligned with the lineage of the promise. In the meantime, through marriage, Esau linked himself with Ishmael's household. This is a picture of us entering into the promises of God. This is also a picture of true worship. Just as we noted earlier about Cain, Esau also chose his own way. However, Jacob went out in search of the promised destiny. Jacob and Rebekah had their problems, but through worship, redemption of this whole mess occurred.

In spite of our scheming and conniving, a sovereign Lord still works to bring about His plans. Our mistakes do not stop the chain forming that is linked to the divine purpose of God. Even with all our carnal ways, God can fashion us to be carriers of His promises. He can position us at the right place at the right time and draw us into His presence. Because the Lord views events from a heavenly perspective and rules from a position of ascension, He knows how to get everything into proper order so that His purposes on Earth can be accomplished. He fully recognizes the best that is within each of us and leads us so the best can be manifested. This is what happened to Jacob.

The Tranformation of Places

Jacob, fleeing to Haran, perceived the presence of the Lord in a dream and when he woke from his sleep, he said: "Surely the LORD is in this place, and I did not know it. . . . How awesome is this place! This is none other than the house of God, and this is the gate of heaven!" (Gen. 28:16-17). Before the dream, the place had only been a stopping point reached by sunset (see v. 11), but when he awoke it had become holy ground. The presence of God had penetrated into ordinary, profane space in a way that had aroused acute awareness on the part of a human being. The sacred (holy) and profane are united in an experience of worship.

The consciousness of holy presence brings forth a response from those who perceive it. The response is worship and may take many forms. The response may be private and intensely personal, in the form of prayers, confessions, silence and meditative experiences. Jesus, leaving the disciples behind in a place called Gethsemane, went a distance from them to fall on the ground and pray alone to the Father (see Mark 14:32-35). According to Matthew 26:39, He "threw himself on the ground and prayed" (NRSV). According to Luke 22:41, he "knelt down, and prayed" (NRSV). Each of these is a physical posture considered appropriate for worship in prayer.

Jacob's response to God's holy presence was to take the stone he had used for a pillow and to set it up as a pillar, declaring it to be a house of God. Apparently he intended that a temple or sanctuary would be built there. This would be a place where communication could occur between the divine or heavenly realm and the human or earthly realm. The messengers of

God would continually go up and down bearing the petitions of worshipers and the responses of God. Thus Jacob proposed that his personal experience of the presence of God be made available to others.

A Link Between Personal and Corporate Worship

Worship in the Bible moves back and forth between personal and corporate experiences. Personal worship may occur in very private circumstances or may be related to public worship. This is illustrated in the book of Psalms by the shifting back and forth from plural speakers to a singular speaker (see Ps. 44).

Personal worship and corporate worship are mutually interactive. Corporate worship is empowered by personal experience, but personal experience needs affirmation and interpretation in a corporate setting. Thus early Christians were warned not to neglect meeting together in worship "as is the habit of some" (Heb. 10:25, *NRSV*) in order to encourage one another in the faith and in the spiritual life.

A Time and Place for Worship

Worship in the Bible appears in varied forms. Times and places are among the major factors. Worship, especially of the corporate type, normally takes place according to some sort of schedule or calendar. There are times and seasons for worship, even though in the Bible God is present with His people at all times.

A sharpened awareness of the divine presence may result from intensive exercises of worship during special times and at special places. These occasions and places are also the contexts for religious education and the development and enjoyment of fellowship among worshipers. Thus in ancient Israel there was the divine command that "three times in the year all your males shall appear before the Lord God [and] three times in the year you shall hold a festival for me" (Exod. 23:17,14, *NRSV*). The

Psalms, with expressions of lament, confession, thanksgiving, praise, teaching and celebration, show the breadth of Old Testament worship.

The followers of Jesus, who later became known as Christians, received a rich heritage of worship from Judaism, but the new dynamics of their experience with Christ brought about major changes. The festivals of Passover and Pentecost were retained but in different forms. The Lord's Supper, the crucifixion and the resurrection of Jesus are all closely related to the Passover celebration (see Matt. 26:17,26-28; 1 Cor. 11:23-26). The Christian Easter celebration is a form of Passover. According to Acts 2:1-42, Pentecost was the occasion of a great filling and empowering of the disciples of Jesus by the Holy Spirit—interpreted as a fulfillment of Joel 2:28-32. References in the New Testament (see Acts 20:16; 1 Cor. 16:8) indicate that the early Christians transformed Pentecost into a Christian observance. Many churches have continued to observe it on the seventh Sunday after Easter.

The Festival of Tabernacles or Booths has not been continued in Christian worship except in the related forms of thanksgiving observances and harvest festivals. The Day of Atonement is used theologically to interpret Christ's sacrifice in Hebrews 8—9, but does not seem to have been a regular part of Christian worship, except in the form of penitential periods such as Lent. For Christians, the whole complex of Temple activities, priesthood, sacrifice, Sabbath and sin-cleansing rituals either became obsolete or were reinterpreted—for instance, the Church itself becomes the temple (see 1 Cor. 6:19; Eph. 2:21-22; 1 Pet. 2:9).

This discussion indicates that worship in the Old Testament context was multifaceted and complex. The New Testament and much of the contemporary Christian expression move away from rigid adherence to calendars and places, but the experience of corporate worship is still important.

The Lord in This Place

The awareness of divine presence, however symbolized and realized, is absolutely essential to worship. Like Jacob, every true worshiper becomes aware that "the Lord is in this place!" As in the case of Jacob, the sense of presence may come in private and

---

The heart of Christian worship is the power of Christ's presence in a gathered community of disciples.

---

personal experience. However, the basic pattern is found in the promise of Jesus, according to Matthew 18:20: "For where two or three are gathered in my name, I am there among them" (*NRSV*). The heart of Christian worship is the power of Christ's presence in a gathered community of disciples (see John 14:12-14; Acts 2:43-47; 4:9-12,32-37; 1 Cor. 5:3-4; Rev. 2:1). According to the New Testament, the presence of Christ is especially manifest in the breaking of the bread at the Lord's Supper (see Luke 24:28-32,35). However, the presence of God is not limited to the Supper and may occur wherever and whenever two or three are gathered in the name of Jesus Christ.

Note

1. Kingdom Dynamics, *Spirit Life Bible* (Nashville, TN: Thomas Nelson Publishers, 1991), p. 1602.

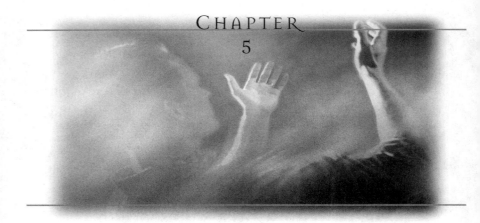

PORTALS OF GLORY

Many of you reading this book are exhausted from all the strife, contention and trials that have been linked to the promise that you have been pursuing. Stop and rest! That's what Jacob did. "Then he dreamed, and behold, a ladder was set up on the earth, and its top reached to heaven; and there the angels of God were ascending and descending on it" (Gen. 28:12). This was really a visitation from God.

In this visitation, God revealed to Jacob that He is the Lord of the past, the present and the future. This brought Jacob into a relationship with the Lord. This caused him to have faith that he could actually grab hold of the promise and blessing that had been spoken over him. This also gave him confidence that he could have a relationship with holy God just as his father and grandfather (Isaac and Abraham) had.

From this experience, Jacob began to worship God personally in the following ways:

1. He acknowledged that the Lord had been in the place with him, even though before that point he could not see Him.
2. He memorialized the place, set up a stone and poured oil on it.
3. He renamed the place Bethel, the House of God.
4. He recognized God as provider.
5. He had a desire to give a portion of what he had back to the Lord.
6. The fear of God began to be a part of his life.
7. He declared that a "gate of heaven" had opened forever in that place. This would link his purpose on Earth into eternity.

In *Worship God!*, Ernest Gentile writes:

The sudden appearance of the heavenly ladders must have seemed to Jacob to be God's invitation to come up into His presence. The transcendent God created a direct way to meet with lowly man. With the ladder, God initiated worship. He made a way for men to come before God. Then, Jacob saw angels model the responsive action of a worshiper. The text speaks of the angels ascending first and then descending. Symbolically, the angels showed what must take place in people's lives if they are to be true, successful servants of the Lord. First, having "seen" the heavenly invitation, they ascend the shining staircase through their worship. Then, after being in the presence of God, they descend the ladder back to Earth to perform acts of service. First they go up to meet with God; then they can go down to the world with ministry of service. Another popular interpretation of this event makes the angels conveyers of God's blessing to man and of man's response to God. Angels do perform such work, but it stresses the text to overemphasize angels as intermediaries between God and men where this is only *one* mediator.[1]

AN OPENING FOR GOD'S PRESENCE ON EARTH

In *The Gate Church*, Pastor Frank Damazio shares on the significance of gates.

The gate in Scripture is a very powerful symbol and is used in connection with a powerful church. Jesus connected the two in Matthew 16:16-18. The word "gate" in the original language can be defined as a structure closing, or enclosure; a large opening through a wall or a barrier created so that people and things can pass to another area, a new area. A gate opens the way into something. It is a passageway or a channel, an avenue. Gates, because of their function in the Old Testament cities, took on a symbolic meaning. Both the prophets and Christ Himself used this symbolism. The Bible describes four functions of city gates during Old Testament times:

1. A place that controlled access and provided strongly fortified protection (see Josh. 2:7; 7:5; Judg. 16:2,3; 18:16,17; 2 Kings 11:6; 14:13).

2. A place where legal or governmental leaders of the city sat to hand down judicial decisions (see Gen. 19:1; Deut. 25:7; 2 Sam. 19:8; Lam. 5:14).

3. A place where business and social functions occurred and where business contracts were made and witnessed (see Gen. 34:24; Ruth 4:1,11; 2 Sam. 15:2).

4. A place where prophetic messages were brought by the prophets and delivered to the elders of the city (see 1 Kings 22:10; 2 Chron. 18:9; Jer. 7:2; 17:19).

The gates are powerful symbols of God's authority over His people. As we see in the book of Isaiah, God's laws that keep His people and the spiritual health of the nation could be symbolized by the usage of this word "gate":

- Open the gates, that the righteous nation which keeps the truth may enter in (26:2).
- Therefore your gates shall be open continually; they shall not be shut day or night, that men may bring to you the wealth of the Gentiles, and their kings in procession (60:11).
- Go through, go through the gates! Prepare the way for the people; build up, build up the highway! Take out the stones, lift up a banner for the peoples! (62:10).

The gates are also symbolic of evil powers that war against the souls of people and against the church that

Christ is building (italics added):

- I said, "In the prime of my life I shall go to the *gates of Sheol*; I am deprived of the remainder of my years" (Isa. 38:10).
- "I will go before you and make the crooked place straight; I will break in pieces the *gates of bronze* and cut the bars of iron" (Isa. 45:2).
- Thus says the LORD of hosts: "The broad walls of Babylon shall be utterly broken, and her high *gates* shall be burned with fire; the people will labor in vain, and the nations, because of the fire; and they shall be weary" (Jer. 51:58).
- "And I also say to you that you are Peter, and on this rock I will build My church, and the *gates of Hades* shall not prevail against it" (Matt. 16:18).[2]

GATES OPEN FOR THE KING OF GLORY

Lift up your heads, O you gates! And be lifted up, you everlasting doors! And the King of glory shall come in. Who is this King of glory? The LORD strong and mighty, the LORD mighty in battle. Lift up your heads, O you gates! Lift up, you everlasting doors! And the King of glory shall come in. Who is this King of glory? The LORD of hosts, He is the King of glory (Pss. 24:7-10).

This is a time to open the gates for the King to enter. The King with His procession is approaching the gate. He asks for entry. The doorkeeper asks, "Who is it that is approaching the gate?" The password is shouted back: "The LORD, strong and mighty, the LORD mighty in battle." This gains Him immediate entry. Who is this King of Glory? He is the Lord of Hosts, Yahweh Sabaoth. He is the captain of all the angelic armies, the armies of Israel, the hosts of nations, ruler of everything in heaven and on Earth. When that heavenly portal opens, we allow this King access in our life, city, corporate worship or nation. Open the portals of glory so He may come in.

THE POWER OF AGREEMENT

In *The Future War of the Church*, Rebecca Wagner Sytsema and I wrote the following concerning heaven and Earth agreeing:

> The power of the Third Day Church will be like none we have known before. . . . Let's take a look at heaven and Earth, and how God is bridging the gap between the two:
>
> **The Third Heaven**
> As we think about heaven, we are more than likely pondering the "third heaven" (2 Cor. 12:2). This is the place where God the Father is seated on His throne and Jesus is seated next to Him. Jesus intimately knows what is on the Father's heart, and we know that from this place at the right hand of God Jesus makes intercession for us (see Rom. 8:34).
>
> Ephesians 1 and 2 are beautiful passages on our inheritance in the Lord and how we are positioned to sit together in heavenly places with Jesus (see Eph. 2:6). This is the place where there is no obstruction to God's will being fully carried out. This is the place we receive our marching orders.

When Jesus ascended to this place He gave gifts to the human race. We find these gifts listed in Ephesians 4:11 with "some to be apostles, some prophets, some evangelists, and some pastors and teachers." He gave

> **H**e gave these gifts to equip the saints for the work of the ministry and for the building up of the Body of Christ.

these gifts to equip the saints for the work of the ministry and for the building up of the Body of Christ. He gave these gifts to produce unity of the faith in the knowledge of Himself and He continues to release revelation so we will not be tossed to and fro by the craftiness and trickery of the enemy. He is also releasing revelation that will cause us to "grow up" into His headship. All of this is occurring from Jesus' place in the Throne Room in the third heaven.

The First Heaven
We live in our physical bodies here in the earthly realm—a place that we can see, touch and feel. This universe in which we live, which includes the moon and the galaxies of stars and planets may be called the first heaven. Through Christ's death and resurrection, we here on earth have access to communicate beyond this universe and into the realm of the third heaven where God is seated. That is what we call prayer.

Psalm 24 says, "The earth is the Lord's and the fullness thereof." So He also rules the earthly realm. When Jesus went to the cross and then overcame the grave, He broke the headship of Satan in this realm. He then set a structure in place on Earth with a gifted government and army (the Church) to enforce His headship.

The Second Heaven

So if we live on Earth but have access to heavenly places through prayer, why is God's will not always done on Earth as it is in heaven? The answer lies in the second heaven where Satan, the "prince of the power of the air" (Eph. 2:2), and his demons contest God's reign and His angels. Satan is the prince of this world (see John 12:31; 14:30; 16:11).

The word "world" is *cosmos* in the Greek. In Matthew 4:8 we find, "The devil took Him up on an exceedingly high mountain, and showed Him all the kingdoms of the world and their glory." The kingdoms of this world have been arranged in such a way that they have an enticing glory about them; this *cosmos* region has the ability to entrap.

The prince of this world is also known as the god of this age:

> The god of this age has blinded the minds of unbelievers, so that they cannot see the light of the gospel of the glory of Christ, who is the image of God (2 Cor. 4:4, *NIV*).

The enemy attempts to block heaven's will from being done on Earth through a demonic hierarchy that is positioned between us and the third heaven (see Eph. 2:2). This hierarchy establishes a ruler as the strongman. The strongman rules and reigns over a kingdom of dark spirits. We find a listing of this hierarchy—principalities, powers, rulers of darkness of this age and spiritual hosts of wickedness in the heavenly places—in Ephesians 6:12.

This hierarchy gains legal right to block heaven's will on Earth through our own rebellion against God and our complicity with the devil's agenda. Satan gains access to us and to entire territories through individual and corporate sin. In such an individualistic society it may be difficult for us to grasp that we, as a society, are held responsible in the eyes of God for corporate sin. Just as in our own lives and in the generations of our family, sin can also be an opening for Satan to establish strongholds that directly oppose God's plan for a territory. The following are a few examples of corporate sin that can give Satan legal right in a region or in our lives.

Idolatry

Idolatry is that place where we have physically or spiritually bowed down and exalted something—whether it be a carved image or the likeness of anything—higher than God (see Exod. 20:3,4). Many places in the world today are being held captive by the enemy because of idolatry. As a result, Satan has legal right to blind the eyes of unbelievers from the glorious gospel of Jesus Christ.

Bloodshed

The first recorded murder was that of Cain's killing his brother, Abel. God said to Cain, "What have you done? The voice of your brother's blood cries out to Me from the ground" (Gen. 4:10). From this we see that bloodshed affects the very land on which the violence occurred. As the blood of violence penetrates the ground, the prince of the power of the air gains rights to the land. Curses on physical land often gain a foothold through violence and bloodshed.

Immorality

The classic biblical example of how immorality can affect entire territories is . . . Sodom and Gomorrah. Immorality and perversity had so overtaken those cities that God could not even find 10 righteous men within their walls. Any redemptive plan that God had for those cities was wiped out as everyone, including the children, were destroyed. . . .

Covenant breaking

During the reign of King David, a great famine came on the land. When David inquired of the Lord concerning this famine, God said to him, "It is because of Saul and his bloodthirsty house, because he killed the Gibeonites" (2 Sam. 21:1). The Gibeonites were a group of people who had entered into covenant with Israel in the days of Joshua. This covenant guaranteed their safety. Yet Saul broke covenant with the Gibeonites by murdering many of them and planning for the massacre of the rest.

As a result, famine came on the land as God removed His blessing and Satan was allowed access. The famine did not strike immediately but rather came when a new king had come to power. This should be a wake-up call for the United States where more than 350 treaties with Native Americans have been broken. . . .

Breaking Through the Second Heaven

The only entity on Earth with the power to break strongholds of Satan and break through his domain in the second heaven is the Church. While we have always had the tools, within the past few decades we have come to a greater understanding of the spiritual warfare that is necessary to destroy the strategies and structures the enemy has in place in the second heaven.

The only entity on Earth with the power to break strongholds of Satan is the Church.

God is establishing a new authority in His church to break through to the third heaven, gain the heart of God, and carry that revelation back to Earth where we can accomplish His will. As we do, we will change the very atmosphere around us—God's will being done on Earth as it is in heaven. This is what we pray for every time we pray the Lord's Prayer!

However, many of us try to avoid the second heaven. Revelation 12:7 says, "And war broke out in heaven:

Michael and his angels fought with the dragon; and the dragon and his angels fought." Dick Eastman writes about the casting down of Satan that results from a great battle between the hosts of heaven and the hordes of hell, as depicted in the passage:

> In this battle, heaven's warriors force Satan and his demons forever from the heavenly realm. But we must note that victory is not achieved solely by the angels, but also by believers' use of spiritual weapons. The angels fight, but God's saints provide the "firepower." This is clearly shown by v. 11, "They overcame him by the blood of the Lamb and by the word of their testimony." The angels did not overcome the Accuser alone; the saints were in partnership through prayer-warfare; the angels were God's means for administering the victory, which prayer enforced. Notice the mention of Michael, the archangel (v. 7, one of four places where he is mentioned in Scripture). In each mention, spiritual warfare is clearly implied. This is true in Daniel 10 where Michael's involvement in battle to victory is the direct result of Daniel's fasting and prayer.[3]

HOW LAND CAN REJOICE

Alistair Petrie writes:

> Land takes on characteristics based on what we do on it, both good and bad. Land can be either defiled or blessed by the people who inhabit it. Throughout Scripture we find numerous examples of how the stewards of the day

had a distinct effect on their environment. In Genesis 3:17 we [are informed] that the ground became cursed because of the fallen stewardship of Adam and Eve, and verses 18 and 19 describe the "thorns and thistles" that would now be part of their day-to-day experience as they worked the land.

In Genesis 4, we have an account of Abel's blood crying out from the ground following his murder at the hands of his brother, Cain. The ground was describing the nature of the untimely stewardship. Genesis 4:11-12 shows the effect on Cain, who was "driven from the ground" because of the curse placed on him, and we learn that he would "be a restless wanderer on the earth."

When we worship, an extension of the kingdom of God in heaven begins to manifest on Earth.

Concerning this passage, [Pastor Bob] Beckett states that: "To be a vagabond means to be homeless, and it is a curse. Moving from place to place leaves one with a desperate feeling of not belonging. Under such circumstances there can no change for vision or destiny to take root. But the ground has been crying out for justice!"[4]

When we worship we see a manifestation of God's justice into the iniquitous patterns on Earth.

Angelic visitation and glory are linked with people. Therefore, healing the land will be connected with individuals.

When we worship, an extension of the kingdom of God in heaven begins to manifest on Earth. Petrie goes on to elaborate on the seven blessings of God that begin to rest on the land:

1. **Ecological health**: I will send you rain in its season, and the ground will yield its crops and the trees of the field their fruit (Lev. 26:4).
2. **Economic health**: Your threshing will continue until grape harvest and the grape harvest will continue until planting, and you will eat all the food you want and live in safety in your land (Lev. 26:5).
3. **Personal security**: I will grant peace in the land, and you will lie down and no one will make you afraid (Lev. 26:6).
4. **Civil security**: I will remove savage beasts from the land, and the sword will not pass through your country (Lev. 26:6).
5. **International security**: You will pursue your enemies, and they will fall by the sword before you. Five of you will chase a hundred, and a hundred of you will chase ten thousand (Lev. 26:7-8).
6. **Honor and growth**: I will look upon you with favor and make you fruitful and increase your numbers, and I will keep my covenant with you (Lev. 26:9).
7. **Innovation and creativity**: You will still be eating last year's harvest when you will have to move it out to make room for the new (Lev. 26:10).

God gives further promises to His people for their obedience: I will put my dwelling place among you, and I will not abhor you. I will walk among you and be your God, and you will be my people. I am the LORD your God, who brought you out of Egypt so that you would no longer be slaves to the Egyptians; I broke the bars of your yoke and enabled you to walk with heads held high (Lev. 26:11-13). These blessings could also be termed the seven transformation principles that are being witnessed in our day around the world. As communities of all sizes are cleansed of their sin and fallen stewardship, these transformation principles are being displayed in their social, political, economic and spiritual aspects.[5]

THE CONFLICT OF COVENANT

This is a time to pursue personal, corporate, territorial and generational breakthrough! Biblically, the year always starts with Rosh Hoshana. Most people do not understand time very well, since they do not understand the earthly time frame the Bible reflects. In September 2001, we saw the world shift into a new mind-set. With the airplanes crashing into the Pentagon and World Trade Center buildings we entered into a season of war. We must shift now into a mind-set of victory and advancement.

This is a season where God is judging nation after nation over how they confess to be aligned with His covenant plan. For instance, in the United States we profess to be a Christian nation. That means we are grafted into the vine of Abraham's covenant. This covenant was fulfilled and made available to us by the Lord Jesus Christ when He went to the Cross.

This covenant is now being severely tested. The antichrist system is now being seen by the world. This system hates anything to do with God's sovereign covenant with the land and nation of Israel. The antichrist system hates anyone who professes to have Jesus Christ within them. Such a person is a threat to the enemy. In September 2001, we entered into a historical season. In Hebraic time it was the year 5762. This actually means the beginning of wars.[6] I believe there is always a time cycle of seven years. This next seven years of training and confrontation will cause God's remnant people to do great exploits for Him. This season, when mastered before the Lord, will cause an awesome release of covenant blessings. The way we can be victorious in this season is to worship Jehovah God like we have never worshiped Him before.

THE BLESSINGS OF THE COVENANT

We can see many blessings manifested on Earth in this season. We are entering into covenant conflict, which means that we are warring to see these blessings spread throughout the earthly realm. Psalm 24:1 declares that the "earth is the LORD's, and the fulness thereof" (*KJV*). God has a plan of fullness. We must go to war to see this fullness manifested. When we open the portals of

What goes on in a spiritual war many times manifests naturally.

heaven, those blessings that have been shut up and unable to be seen will be manifested on Earth.

One of the key points that I shared in public at the time of the new millennium was that this would be a season for us to put on a war mantle. Often I was asked if I thought we would go into a physical war. I always said yes and explained that I felt that a physical war was imminent and would occur by September 2001. I actually prophesied this in October 2000.

When I communicated this prophecy, I met some resistance because it was difficult for people to understand the relationship between spiritual war and physical war. What goes on in a spiritual war many times manifests naturally (see Rev. 12). A corporate spiritual war affects every aspect of natural society: religion, politics (legal and military), economics and education. Therefore, God raises up *worshiping intercessors* in each one of these arenas of power. From a spiritual point of view we have seen a shift in society. We have seen the beginning of war.

The tragedy of the World Trade Center and Pentagon attacks were physical manifestations of the season ahead. As two commercial airplanes with suicide pilots approached the World Trade Center and another headed toward the Pentagon (and a fourth crashed in Pennsylvania), the world as we knew it changed. The resulting crashes and disintegration of the two towers and the loss of approximately 3,000 lives propelled the world, including the United States, into an unprecedented season of conflict. Pastor Dutch Sheets wrote the following:

> As we all observe and mourn the results of the recent terrorist attacks on America, the response of the Body of Christ and the way in which we pray could very well determine whether our nation turns toward God or away from God. Sorrow can lead either to bitterness, which perpetuates greater defilement (see Heb. 12:15), or to repentance resulting in salvation (see 2 Cor. 7:10). Measured, accurate and biblical responses from those of us representing God are critical.

How Should We Define the Events?

Great caution should be exercised in using the word "judgment" to *define* these events. Many Christians understand that America has been experiencing a degree of judgment for some time—sin has wages (see Rom. 6:23). But most biblical judgment is the inevitable, built-in consequence of sin, not the direct hand of God. He did not pronounce curses after Adam and Eve's fall because He was an angry God who loves to curse sinners. He did so because of the inherent results of their actions. And He did it while covering their nakedness and promising redemption, a redemption involving great sacrificial love on His part—the incarnation and death of His Son (see Gen. 3:15).

Also, rather than the direct hand of God, judgments are often simply the result of forfeiting God's favor and protection. Jonah 2:8 tells us: "Those who cling to worthless idols forfeit the grace that could be theirs."

A careful and compassionate explanation of reaping, or the consequences of sin and of turning from God, should be our definition of the events. I would advise not even using the term "judgment" because the world will probably not hear anything else we say. Other pertinent Scriptures that could be used to explain the fruit of sin and the forfeiting of God's protection are:

Psalm 127:1-2: "Unless the Lord builds the house, they labor in vain who build it. Unless the Lord guards the city, the watchman keeps awake in vain. It is vain for you to rise up early, to retire late, to eat the bread of painful labors; for He gives to His beloved even in his sleep."

Proverbs 14:34: "Righteousness exalts a nation, but sin is a disgrace to any people."

Proverbs 28:13: "He who conceals his transgressions will not prosper, but he who confesses and forsakes them will find compassion."

Isaiah 59:1-2: "Behold, the Lord's hand is not so short that it cannot save; neither is His ear so dull that it cannot hear. But your iniquities have made a separation between you and your God, and your sins have hidden His face from you, so that He does not hear."

Luke 13:34-35: "O Jerusalem, Jerusalem, the city that kills the prophets and stones those sent to her! How often I wanted to gather your children together, just as a hen gathers her brood under her wings, and you would not have it! Behold, your house is left to you desolate; and I say to you, you shall not see Me until the time comes when you say, 'Blessed is He who comes in the name of the Lord!'"

Luke 19:41-44: "And when He approached, He saw the city and wept over it, saying, 'If you had known in this day, even you, the things which make for peace! But now they have been hidden from your eyes. For the days shall come upon you when your enemies will throw up a bank before you, and surround you, and hem you in on every side, and will level you to the ground and your children within you, and they will not leave in you one stone upon another, because you did not recognize the time of your visitation.'"

What Should Be Our Message?

Our *message*, therefore, must be one of carefully balanced *grace* and *truth* (see John 1:17). God's desire is always to forgive and redeem, not to destroy. Our gospel includes—in addition to the incarnation, death and resurrection of Jesus—two other very important messages: repentance from sin and grace to the repentant. Christ came for the sick, not the healthy; to seek and save the lost, not the found. "For God so loved the world that He gave His only begotten Son. . . . For God did not send the Son into the world to judge the world, but that the world should be saved through Him" (John 3:16-17).

This message of grace need not leave out the consequences of sin, but as it is shared it must be laced with hope and with God's merciful heart. His desire is to *turn* us from our sin, not *destroy* us for it (see 2 Chron. 7:14). He is "slow to anger and abundant in lovingkindness" (Ps. 86:15). At times He actually announced judgments through tears (see Luke 19:41-44), and the Scriptures are clear that He takes no pleasure in the judgment of the wicked (see Ezek. 18:23-32).

God forgave a harlot named Rahab, then gave her a prominent plan in Israel's history as the great-great-grandmother of King David and a part of the lineage leading to Christ. He was willing to spare Sodom; He did spare Nineveh when she repented. And on another occasion He unsuccessfully sought for an intercessor so He could spare Israel (see Ezek. 22:30-31).

So, yes, our message must call sinners to repentance—we cannot compromise truth—but God's heart of compassion, mercy and grace *must* fill the message with hope. "Return to Me and I will return to you" (Mal. 3:7) should be the heart of our message. The result of the returning will be healing and restoration.

What Should Our Attitude Be?

Rather than one of harshly announcing judgment, our *attitude* must be one of compassion and mourning. Like Jeremiah and Christ Himself, we must be able to explain the results of sin through heartfelt tears (see Lam. 1:16; 2:11; 3:48-49; Luke 19:41-44). Too often the world perceives our attitude toward the consequences of others' sins—whether the death of an abortionist or AIDS in a homosexual—as callous or even smug gladness. Satan is an expert at distorting the perception of Christ and the Church in the eyes of the world. We must be wiser than he and make certain the Christ we reveal—the One who loves sinners—is accurate.

We must also be quick to acknowledge our responsibility in the condition of America:

- Some immature leaders, including prophets immature in their calling, have brought forth only harshness and condemnation in their attempts to call the nation to repentance. This turns the hearts of unbelievers *away from* God.
- On the other hand, many pastors and caregivers have overemphasized mercy and grace, refusing to call individuals to biblical accountability.
- The Church in America as a whole has preached a "what's in it for me" humanistic gospel, leaving out the message of taking up our cross and laying down our lives. This has produced great compromise and lukewarmness in the Body of Christ.
- Many of us have failed to truly care for and minister to the poor and hurting, and in general have lacked genuine compassion.
- We in the Church have decried materialism, greed and the love of money as a great part of the problem in America, while fewer than 20% of us even tithe, let alone give sacrificial

offerings. Our hypocrisy contributes to the problem.
- We have failed to pray as we should for government leaders and the lost.

We must acknowledge that judgment begins at our house (see 1 Pet. 4:17) and do our share of the repenting.[7]

A SPIRITUAL JACOB'S LADDER

Everyone knows that the United States went into trauma and mourning on September 11, 2001. Much of the world mourned with us. On March 11, 2002, we "remembered" this tragic time by an hour of prayer and silence. Also, where the World Trade Center had stood, two lights permeated the heavens.

Bill Yount writes:

On March 11, as the bright lights were turned on in the darkness representing the Twin Towers, I heard a rumbling in the heavens as though New York City had captured the attention of Heaven—as though the light could be seen from the Portals of Heaven. Immediately I saw Angels beginning to descend down upon these light rays like they were a "Jacob's Ladder." As though Angels were waiting in line for the moment the rays of light would be turned on . . . creating an open heaven for Angels on assignment to descend. I heard the Father speak to these ministering Angels. "These Rays of Light are man's ways of reaching upward to me. Though they don't know me they are seeking for a 'Ray of Hope' in their darkness. WE MUST GO DOWN!" As these Angels began to descend downward, the "Twin Towers" of Light eventually became covered solid with Angels from top to bottom. I sensed many of these Angels were the ones that were present on Sept. 11th and had ushered in many of the dying into the presence of the Lord. Now these same Angels were descending downward once again to minister and bring comfort and hope to those who had suffered great loss of loved ones (Heb. 1:14), "Are they not all ministering spirits, sent forth to minister for them who shall be heirs of salvation?" There was a definite assignment given to these Angels to war against the hopelessness of life and influence many to turn to Jesus, their only hope. I heard the Father's voice speak into New York City and America, Isaiah 60:1:

ARISE [from the depression and prostration in which circumstances have kept you; rise to a new life]! Shine [be radiant with the glory of the Lord]; for your light is to come, and the glory of the Lord is risen upon you! For behold, darkness shall cover the earth, and dense darkness all peoples; but the Lord shall arise upon you [O Jerusalem], and His glory shall be seen on you. And nations shall come to your light, and kings to the brightness of your rising.[8]

The Light of His Countenance

When the world seems dark
And the shadows are deep:
Though the walls tower o'er us
We can walk the unknown
In the light of his countenance.

Buildings can come down
While threatening with fear
Through the deeds of evil.
Yet we fearlessly follow His map
By the light of His countenance.

The tide is turning; we will prevail
As we move reclaiming territory
Claimed by he who fell from grace;
Who roared threateningly, but now must retreat
Under the light of His countenance.

Intercessors are arising, uniting
While the tsunami of youth is bulging upward
Drawing all streams of believers into the strong
    currents
All coming together in powerful overcoming strength
Fully *empowered by the light of His countenance.*

His Church, the Body of Christ shall prevail
Filled by the power of His love
Engulfing the earth,
Covering it with
The light of His countenance.[9]

Notes

1. Ernest B. Gentile, *Worship God!* (Portland, OR: City Bible Publishing, 1994), p. 90.
2. Frank Damazio, *The Gate Church* (Portland, OR: City Bible Publishing, 2000), pp. 1-3.
3. Chuck D. Pierce and Rebecca Wagner Sytsema, *The Future War of the Church* (Ventura, CA: Renew Books, 2001), pp. 77-84.
4. Alistair Petrie, *Releasing Heaven on Earth* (Grand Rapids, MI: Chosen Books, 2000), p. 42.
5. Ibid., pp. 200-201.

6. Yitzchak Ginsburg, "A Torah Message for the Month of Tishrei, Rosh HaShana 5762, The Year of a Sign of Blessing," *The Inner Dimension*, http://www.inner.org/times/tishrei/tishrei62.thm (accessed August 12, 2002).

7. Dutch Sheets, "A Biblical Response to the Terrorist Attacks on America for the Purpose of Prayer and Evangelism," September 14, 2001.

8. Bill Yount, "Twin Tower Lights Create a 'Spiritual' Jacob's Ladder," *OurChurch.Com*, www.ourchurch.com/member/b/BillYount/ (accessed March 12, 2002).

9. Keat Wade, "The Light of His Countenance," score, 2001.

THE FAITH TO ASCEND

In biblical accounts, war has always had a religious significance. Since Israel was the firstfruits of God and His inheritance, the priests reminded their armies that Yahweh was with them to fight their battles (see Deut. 20:1-4). To open a campaign, or to enter an engagement, the priests performed sacrificial rites (see 1 Sam. 7:8-10; 13:9). If the people *prepared for war* and made the appropriate sacrifices to a Holy God, this would *sanctify* the war (see Jer. 6:4; 22:7; 51:27-28; Joel 3:9; Mic. 3:5).

Isaiah 13:3 declares that Yahweh gathers His host and summons to battle His "consecrated ones" (*NASB*). The priests, consecrated by the sacrifices offered before the war, actually were the forerunners in battle.

The Lord is calling out His forerunners today. There is a holy sanctification going on in the Body as He prepares us to stand against the forces that hold captive our families, churches and cities. If we are to go forth in war, then we do not want to go without the Lord at the lead. He is Emmanuel, *God with Us*!

PREPARE WITH WORSHIP

According to Isaiah 7, a coalition had been formed to make war against Judah. Syria and a faction in Israel had aligned itself to force Judah into a direction that was not God's will. The Lord sent Isaiah and his son, Shear-Jashub ("A Remnant Shall Return"), to prophesy to the king. This son's name was a sign that even though judgment would reign there would always be a remnant. Isaiah then began to prophesy that the Lord Himself would give a sign to Ahaz: "Behold, the virgin shall conceive and bear a Son, and shall call His name Emmanuel" (v. 14). God was saying that the sign would be an assurance that in the midst of adversity there would always be hope. I believe it is key for us to remember that God longs to be with us at all times. *If we will worship Him, He will be there to help us!*

A Word from God

When my son Daniel was seven years old he came to his mother and me with a question: "What is anthrax?" We both were astonished that a seven-year-old boy would ask such a question. My stepfather (Daniel's grandfather) had cows and land, so I assumed that he had mentioned the issue of anthrax occurring in a natural context. However, when my wife and I questioned Daniel over where he had heard the word "anthrax," he said, "The Lord spoke it to me and said it is coming to America." I explained to him what anthrax was. We have always been honest with our kids, so I just laid it all out on the line. This caused him to fear that it might come upon him. When he would touch something, he would immediately wash his hands. This threw us into a crisis as a family.

In my quiet time one morning I began to seek the Lord, asking Him how He would pull us out of this awkward situation and bring freedom and confidence to Daniel. The Spirit of God said: "This will not be an issue in Daniel's life until he is 20 years old." At breakfast that morning when he began to obsessively discuss anthrax with us, I told him what the Lord had said. Pam gave me that look that said Why in the world would you say this so I have to live with his obsessive fear for the next 13 years? Nothing really changed, except that I had heard God.

Respond in Worship

When I do not know what to do, I either worship or ask God what I can give. I find that I can begin to hear Him when I begin to worship, and He will always tell me where to give. Then I can hear Him on the issues that burden my heart. That night when I put Daniel to bed, I said to him, "Let's worship." We listened to a Psalty audiocassette and sang along. At the end of the music, I said to Daniel, "You know how much Mom and I love you. We have tried every way we know to help you get through the fear of what God has shown you. Perfect love casts out all fear. God does not give you the spirit of fear. Therefore, ask the Lord to show you how much He loves you. Since we've worshiped, is there anything you want to ask the Lord?" Daniel replied, "I've been trying to catch a butterfly all week, and I've not been able to."

As any good parent, I wanted to go out and find every butterfly I could find and put them all in his room so that when he awakened, they would be surrounding him. However, I knew I could not do that. I had to trust the Lord. The next morning, when he got up and we were sitting outside, he still feared anthrax. While I was praying for him before I left for work, an interesting thing happened. A butterfly flew into our yard and landed upon Daniel's shirt. He cupped his hands around the butterfly and looked up at the Lord and said, "Because You have shown me how much You love me, I'm just going to set this butterfly free." This was quite a moment.

Anthrax Comes to America

On Daniel's 20th birthday, the headlines in the newspapers in America read Anthrax Strikes America. Daniel now works for the law enforcement agency in our region and is enrolled in the police academy. I was traveling and called him on his birthday.

Worship causes us to experience the Father's love.

Remembering God's word about anthrax, I asked Daniel how he was doing. He said, "Dad, since we worshiped that night and God revealed His love to me the next day, I have never questioned His love over protecting me in the midst of this particular crisis." He had received faith that would last him the next 13 years of his life and extend into the future.

Worship causes us to experience the Father's love. Faith works by love. As we worship, faith is released.

THE ABILITY OF GOD

I heard these words in my spirit: "God is able!" The Holy Spirit seemed to be beckoning me to pray for God's people. In my prayers I was to declare *God's ability to make each one of us able to overcome.* I could perceive that many people were hearing the voice of the Lord; however, our hearing was not turning into the necessary faith to overcome. I asked the Lord what the problem was, and He said the following: "My people are to go from faith to faith. They are struggling in their going. They have weak faith. Their expectations and hope of Me performing future happenings that will produce favorable outcomes in their lives are being sidetracked by circumstances. These circumstances are keeping them from entering into MY creative power. This new vigor and strength that I can release will catapult them into this next dimension. I AM ABLE. LEAN NOT ON YOUR OWN ABILITIES, FOR I CAN ENABLE YOU."

Faith should be growing and steadfast. Faith should be abiding and continuing. Faith should be producing work in God's kingdom. I see that we have grown anxious in the cares of this world. We have fallen into fear of failure, fear of harm, fear of abandonment and fear of the future. We have forgotten God's ability to bless. God is able to give us the faith to get there!

One meaning of the word "endure" is to repair a broken foot so we can step forward, continue on our journeys and possess the promises God has for us.

Stand and worship! Let the Lord shod your feet with peace. May any place in your spiritual walk where peace has been broken be mended. Worship and continue on your journey to prophetic fulfillment. "And God is able to make all grace abound toward you, that you, always having all sufficiency in all things, may have an abundance for every good work" (2 Cor. 9:8). Receive His superabundant grace so that every hindrance that is in your path that is resisting you from reaching your "there" will be overcome and your life cycle will be fulfilled.

THE ROLE OF FAITH IN WORSHIP

In general, faith is the persuasion of the mind that a certain statement is true (see Phil. 1:27; 2 Thess. 2:13). We must see that when a thing is true then it is worthy of our trust, which is the primary principle at work here. As we saw when we looked at the "layers" in Amos 9:6 earlier, faith has levels or degrees. We go though layers of dark resistance until we come into full assurance that what we seek will be manifested.

Faith comes through teaching, reading and hearing the Word (see Rom. 10:14-17), which releases knowledge. Knowledge is an essential element in all faith and is sometimes noted as an equivalent to faith (see John 10:38; 1 John 2:3). However, faith differs from knowledge because it includes assent. This is an act of the will through worship. To ascend in worship and receive truth is the essence of faith. The ultimate ground on which our assent to any revealed truth rests is the veracity of our seeking and touching God. The accuracy or precision of how we operate on Earth depends on our ascent by faith into His Throne Room.

DIFFERENT DIMENSIONS OF FAITH

There are layers of faith, each with a dimension of revelation. Here are different types of faith levels and their corresponding releases.

1. **Historical Faith**. This type of faith is where we apprehend and ascend based upon certain statements and historical accounts that have occurred in history. We read a fact from history, and it causes faith to rise up. A good example is the revival that occurred in Wales at the beginning of the twentieth century. This revival was characterized by incredible music and manifestation of healing. The world was greatly affected by this manifestation of God on Earth. Therefore, when we read about it in history, we say, "Do it again, Lord!"

2. **Saving Faith.** Faith and eternal life are inseparably connected. The Assembly's Shorter Catechism says

this, "Faith in Jesus Christ is a saving grace, whereby we receive and rest upon Him alone for salvation, as He is offered to us in the gospel." From the time the Lord clothed Adam and Eve after the Fall, saving faith becomes the object of the revealed Word of God. This special act of faith unites us to Christ (see John 7:38; Acts 16:31). This act of faith justifies sinners before God (see John 3:16-36; Rom. 3:22,25). This type of faith knows that Jesus is our mediator concerning all of our problems. This type of faith causes us to trust in and rest in Christ for redemption. This type of faith embraces Jesus as Savior. This type of faith renews our wills. Worship is a response of the will of man back to its creator. When we respond to our creator, this is a type of worship that causes us, even as sinners, to take our assigned place in time and creation. We actually begin to fall in with what God is doing on Earth in our generation and align ourselves with it. There is no particular merit in this faith other than that it releases grace to us that aligns us with eternity. This type of faith rests immediately on "thus sayeth the Lord": we hear the Word, the good news, and we respond accordingly. This good news lets us know we can have eternal life. This good news then begins to show us that we can begin to live an abundant life here on Earth. This good news secures us from condemnation and justifies us before God. This type of faith gives us peace with God and begins to sanctify our life (see John 6:37,40; 10:27,28; Rom. 8:1).

3. **Temporary Faith**. Temporary faith occurs when the Holy Spirit quickens us. All of a sudden, we have truth and influence so we can make the right decision. However, this type of faith must be grounded. I see

individuals have a quickening touch from God, and then, as the Word says, this type of faith gets crowded out with the cares of the world or the birds of the field begin to remove what has been quickened in them (see Matt. 13). This type of faith awakens us, but does not keep us awake. Only by worshiping after we have been quickened can we begin to establish this quickening within our spirit.

4. **Supernatural Faith**. John Dickson has a *gift of faith*. This is a supernatural manifestation of a holy God within our spirit man. This usually comes through worship. This type of faith has visible evidence. This faith goes beyond natural faith and saving faith into supernatural trust where no doubt can shake us from what we have heard. Pam, my wife, also operates in this. I worship on a daily basis and really am more project oriented and walk in the war of faith. John or Pam will be worshiping and begin to pray about the issue that's in their heart and all of a sudden know that God has taken care of that issue. This is supernatural faith. They look at the person that they are praying for, and that person is already healed. This might not manifest for another year, but in their heart, it's done. I usually have to war through the year until the manifestation comes.

5. **War of Faith**. There is a progression of faith that comes, I believe, as we worship. The more we ascend, the greater release of faith comes into our spirit man. You have an issue or a burden or a project that you are praying through. You worship and get a piece of the puzzle. God speaks to you during worship. From His voice you war through the next season, and then you gain new ground. You worship more, and you get

more revelation. From this revelation, you war. First Timothy 1:18 reads, "According to the prophecies . . . concerning you, that by them you may wage the good warfare." You gain revelation. When you war,

---

> The more we ascend,
> the greater release of faith comes
> into our spirit man.

---

you gain more revelation. When you war, eventually you see the project or building completed. I call this the Nehemiah type of faith.

6. **Overcoming Faith**.

Then I heard a loud voice saying in heaven, "Now salvation, and strength, and the kingdom of our God, and the power of His Christ have come, for the accuser of our brethren, who accused them before our God day and night, has been cast down. And they overcame him by the blood of the Lamb and by the word of their testimony, and they did not love their lives to the death" (Rev. 12:10-11).

There is an ongoing warfare in the earthly realm. Because the Kingdom has come and is within us, we have the ability to overcome our enemies. When the sound of heaven is imparted into our spirit man, faith arises. This is the sound of triumph. It's the sound of the blood. It's the sound of authority. It's the sound of redemption. It's the sound of overcoming. Once we appropriate this sound, the victory of the finished work of Christ begins to manifest.

7. **Manifested or Glory Faith.**

He who has My commandments and keeps them, it is he who loves Me. And he who loves Me will be loved by My Father, and I will love him and manifest Myself to him (John 14:21).

To "manifest" is to cause to shine. To "manifest" means to reveal, appear or come into view. Therefore, God manifests His presence to us, and we feel His weightiness upon us and in our midst. I call this "glory faith." We are actually clothed with heaven's clothing—His glory. This produces honor, splendor, power, release of wealth, authority, fame, magnificence, dignity and excellence. This is the type of faith that made the individuals of the faith chapter, Hebrews 11, who they were. This is the type of faith we should actually wear in the earthly realm. I believe this is the type of faith that will cover Earth in the latter days.

INSIDE THE THRONE ROOM

Seeing then that we have a great High Priest who has passed through the heavens, Jesus the Son of God, let us hold fast our confession. For we do not have a High Priest who cannot sympathize with our weaknesses, but was in all points tempted as we are, yet without sin. Let us therefore come boldly to the throne of grace, that we

may obtain mercy and find grace to help in time of need
(Heb. 4:14-16).

To "come boldly" means don't be reserved and to come in with
frankness and full-open speech. Many of us do not come into
the Throne Room boldly because we forget we are approaching
a throne of grace. We think of the Throne Room as judgment.
We obtain mercy for everything we have ever done in the past.
Then we gain new grace and faith for our present circumstances. We also gain so much faith that it propels us into the
future.

Not only can we come boldly into the Throne Room by wor-
shiping God, but worship enthrones God (see Ps. 22:3). Dick
Eastman writes the following in *Heights of Delight: An Invitation to
Intercessory Worship*:

> Today's growing harp and bowl intercessory worship
> movement is precisely this, possibly taken to new
> heights in the pursuit of God. And you can join this
> movement daily. It's simple: Declare in song (worship)
> and prayer (intercession) that God dwells, or is
> enthroned, in every situation. This is the result of all
> this intercessory worship: God *is* being enthroned
> because His people *are* pursuing Him in passionate
> worship as never before. Throne zones *are* being estab-
> lished through the earth where God can dwell in all His
> fullness. Radical, revolutionary intercession is the
> result, and a new climate is being created to transform
> people and nations through fruitful evangelism. And
> this is only the beginning.[1]

The apostle John was probably the last of the original
apostles who walked on Earth. These apostles were responsible

to pass their mantle of revelation from generation to generation.

We find John on the Isle of Patmos, a place on Earth, but ascending into a place in the heavenlies. From this place, he communicated to us revelation and information from heaven and its pattern. This is necessary for us to understand as we advance through the ages. His worshiping heart received sights and sounds from heaven. He saw patterns in heaven that God wanted to manifest in the earth. John saw God enthroned as our omnipotent creator. God showed John His Throne. Everything in heaven revolved around this royal Throne. He saw the living creatures and he saw the elders join in with the living creatures in worship. He then saw Jesus as the conquering lion and the helpless lamb. I like what Ernest Gentile writes in *Worship God*:

> The Lamb is the living Jesus radiant in His glory! The wounds that cause His death gleam as the proof of His saviorhood. . . . Because of His death, Jesus was entitled as the Lamb of God (see John 1:29) to break open the book of destiny and allow God's historical purposes to climax. The precious body and blood of the Lamb appear as the very heart and bosom of God the Father, and as such, are positioned "in the midst of the throne." At first, only the omnipotent, Father-Creator-God was worshiped, but now the atoning, Triumphant-Savior-Son receives worship as well. Heaven reverberates with the passionate and extravagant worship of the heavenly hosts. Cries of "Worthy is the Lamb!" roll through the heavenlies in ever-swelling tones. The words of this great hymn by J. Mountain express in a small measure the sights and sounds of this celestial scene:

'Tis the church triumphant singing
Worthy the Lamb;
Heaven throughout with praises ringing
Worthy the Lamb.
Thrones and powers before Him bending,
Odours sweet with voice ascending,
Swell the chorus never-ending
Worthy the Lamb!

Every kindred, tongue and nation,
Worthy the Lamb;
Join to sing the great salvation,
Worthy the Lamb.
Loud as mighty thunders roaring,
Floods of mighty waters pouring,
Prostrate at His feet adoring,
Worthy the Lamb!

Harps and songs forever sounding
Worthy the Lamb;
Mighty Grace o'er sin abounding
Worthy the Lamb.
By His blood He dearly bought us;
Wand'rings from the fold He sought us,
And to glory safely brought us:
Worthy the Lamb![2]

Psalm 11:4-5 reads, "The LORD is in His holy temple, the LORD's throne is in heaven; His eyes behold, His eyelids test the sons of men. The LORD tests the righteous, but the wicked and the one who loves violence His soul hates." Even though we are being tested in the earthly realm, we have access to the Throne Room to find grace to endure. From this place, we rule with

Him. Even though evil thrones are built on Earth, when we worship a holy God His presence is released to break down every evil structure opposed to His kingdom.

EMBRACE THE GLORY

John worshiped around and before the Throne. He witnessed worship coming out of the Throne. He was right in the midst of the Throne. When he was caught up in heaven, he was in "the glory."

John had greater insights than any man of his generation. He received a clear message that is recorded in Revelation 22:6-11:

> Then he said to me, "These words are faithful and true." And the Lord God of the holy prophets sent His angel to show His servants the things which must shortly take place. "Behold, I am coming quickly! Blessed is he who keeps the words of the prophecy of this book." Now I, John, saw and heard these things. And when I heard and saw, I fell down to worship before the feet of the angel who showed me these things. Then he said to me, "See that you do not do that. For I am your fellow servant, and of your brethren the prophets, and of those who keep the words of this book. Worship God." And he said to me, "Do not seal the words of the prophecy of this book, for the time is at hand. He who is unjust, let him be unjust still; he who is filthy, let him be filthy still; he who is righteous, let him be righteous still; he who is holy, let him be holy still."

What was seen in the Throne Room was not to be sealed up or kept secret from any generation. The revelation coming out of heaven was relevant to all Christians until the Lord comes in ultimate fulfillment of His kingdom plan.

The Word of God declares, "But we all, with unveiled face, beholding as in a mirror the glory of the Lord, are being transformed into the same image *from glory to glory,* just as by the Spirit of the Lord" (2 Cor. 3:18, emphasis added). Through our Lord Jesus' sacrificial death, He made a way for us to go into the Throne Room and experience His glory. We go from one place of glory to another place of glory. Through His death, the veil into the Holy of Holies where His presence dwells was torn in two. God made His presence available to those who would believe in Him. At this point, the Bethel House of God, David's Tabernacle and Solomon's Temple moved from the external building into the very heart of mankind. Therefore, His glory can indwell us and manifest through us. Paul said to the Corinthians, "Do you not know that you are the temple of God and that the Spirit of God dwells in you?" (1 Cor. 3:16). To be filled with faith is to be filled with God's presence.

Who is this King of Glory? The glory of God is the Spirit of God. As we open the gates of our hearts, His glory comes in. I remember the first time I really experienced the glory of God. I was 18, and it was as if His love just surrounded me. Later, when I was 24, I had another incredible meeting with the Lord. I had seen certain sin and iniquitous patterns that had hindered the two prior generations of my family. I write about this in *Possessing Your Inheritance,* in the chapter titled "Understanding Sin and Generational Iniquity."

When we came into relationship with God through Christ, we actually entered into a blood covenant with Him (see Matt. 26:28 and parallels: Mark 14:24; Luke 22:20; 1 Cor. 11:25). In that moment a divine exchange took place. God released the holy blood of Christ to make atonement for our sins. Enormous power is available to us in the blood of Christ beyond our initial salvation. We, however, must choose to appropriate that power just as we did when we first came to Christ—salvation was available to us, but we were not actually saved until we came to God and accepted Christ. Through the power of Christ's blood, we can exchange such things as curses for blessings; guilt for purity; sickness for health; lack for provision; sorrow for joy; slavery for freedom and death for eternal life.[3]

The cleansing power of the blood of the Lord Jesus Christ allows His Spirit to manifest within us, which causes His glory to invade every cell of our being. Hebrews 9:14-15 reports,

How much more shall the blood of Christ, who through the eternal Spirit offered Himself without spot to God, cleanse your conscience from dead works to serve the living God? And for this reason He is the Mediator of the new covenant, by means of death, for the redemption of the transgressions under the first covenant, that those who are called may receive the promise of the eternal inheritance.

On this point, Bob Sorge writes:

The Truth is that God's Glory is disruptive. It's untamed, uncontrollable, unstoppable, and dangerously all-consuming. It destroys agendas, calendars, service orders, songlists, and carefully devised plans. It frustrates, exposes, confounds, and renders powerless the controlling mechanisms of church leaders. Glory is dangerous and revolutionary. It's explosive, undomesticated, volatile, divisive, and invasive. Glory smashes in like a tidal wave, washing away the safety nets and lines of familiarity that have helped us feel secure. The clock might help to establish when the meeting starts, but it's useless in determining when the meeting might stop. Buildings become overcrowded, restrooms can hardly be kept clean, children seem to be everywhere, critics abound, and the neighbors complain.[4]

I know when the glory of God started manifesting in my life. It turned things upside down. I see the same thing in churches.

GLORY VERSUS RELIGION

When the glory of God comes into our midst, things change. The norm is disrupted. I believe going from glory to glory is one of the hardest things we must overcome in Christianity. Once the Lord visits us and manifests His glory, a new order begins. As

> When the glory of God comes into our midst, things change. The norm is disrupted.

Bob Sorge noted, everything is disrupted. To process the disruption of God's glory, leadership must set new administrative procedures in place. These eventually become the methods of the visitation of God's glory. However, when it's time for a new revelation to come forth so that the Church is relevant to the society of its season, God visits again. His glory disrupts again. Our snare is this: We want to keep operating in the methods that we were using in the last manifestation of God's glory.

In Ephesians 6:11, the Word of God instructs us to put on the whole armor of God that we might stand against the wiles, or scheming, of the devil. In the Greek, this word "wiles" is *methodeia* and means the method or trickery that lies in wait. This is how religious spirits compete with and stop the next move of God's glory on Earth. When we do not want to move on and experience what God has for us today, we are tricked into thinking that what we have experienced in the past is good enough. Therefore, the glory of God begins to actually depart from us. We find an example of this in 1 Samuel 4. The leadership and the people had fallen into such disarray that the Ark of the Lord was captured in battle. Phinehas's wife said during her laborious child birth, "The glory has departed" (1 Sam. 4:21).

When we stop moving forward in worship, the awe, glory and presence of God eventually leave. This does not happen suddenly. Usually it starts when we resist change and progresses over time. I believe we lose our desperation for God. We would rather not change and settle for a form of godliness than seek God Himself. We have to remember the principle in 1 Samuel 4. Israel had fallen into disarray because of an ungodly priesthood. This caused the glory of God to depart. However, we see that the presence of God lingered. The Ark of the Covenant of God represented His presence. Eventually, the Ark was captured by the enemy's camp.

Likewise we have access to the glory and the presence of God; yet because we do not recognize and honor His glory and presence in our midst, He allows Himself to be removed.

The First Miracle

I love Jesus' first miracle. I believe we should always go look at the firsts in the Bible—it is from those that we gain our prototypes. Jesus and His disciples are with His mother at a wedding.

His mother encourages Him to do something about the wine running out before the wedding ends. Weddings usually lasted about seven days. So it was always good for the best wine to be drunk first. Then during all the revelry they could bring out the old wine and use that up when no one would notice the wine was not of the same quality as before.

Jesus begins to make a move to reveal His true identity on Earth. John 2:6-7 chronicles the event: "Now there were set there six waterpots of stone, according to the manner of purification of the Jews, containing twenty or thirty gallons a piece. Jesus said to them, 'Fill the waterpots with water.' And they filled them up to the brim." The waterpots were used in a ritualistic ceremonial type of way. Jesus was about to show them a new way of celebration. We all know the story—He changed the water into very good wine.

If we will allow the Lord to break into our ritualistic worship, we will begin to receive the best He has for us. This miracle was the beginning of signs that Jesus did in Cana of Galilee. It allowed the manifestation of His glory and demonstrated His deity and purpose. His disciples began to believe Him, because they had actually seen the glory revealed. God is releasing His glory today. May we receive it in our midst.

THE HEAVENLY HOST

Imagine angels showing up to announce that the glory of God had come to Earth. Angels often precede God's glory; they also follow after it. We are entering into a season of angelic visitation. Already we are probably visited by more angels than we know.

I often travel around the world to share the glory of God. I am thankful angels go before me and are with me as I travel. Marty Cassady, strategic prayer leader for Global Harvest, shares the following story:

My friend and I were in Naples, Italy, on a prayer journey. We had completed everything we had set out to do and realized that we still had one full day left on the trip. As we began to look at the map and pray about what to do on our final day, we both felt that we should visit Pompeii. Since we were staying in a private home and didn't have transportation of our own, our hostess told us which city bus to take to the train station and which train stop we should take for Pompeii. We set out on the day's journey realizing, and yet not quite realizing, how noticeable we must have been on the bus. We were both dressed very casually, but most of those around us on the bus were rather rough looking, to put it mildly. We just knew we had prayed about the decision and felt no hesitation or fear to continue on our journey.

We made it to the train station and got our tickets. Waiting for the train was a bit uncomfortable as the look and demeanor of those around us had taken a turn for the worse. It really did seem to be a very bad section of a city that is known for its lawlessness. Still we were not overly concerned, and we had made up our minds to hold tightly to our purses and mind our own business. We entered the train and the seating was in sections of four seats each with two seats facing two more seats. I will never forget the first time the train stopped to allow passengers on and off. In walked a very American-looking gentleman dressed in a pair of tan khaki slacks, a white golf shirt and a navy blue blazer, wearing Dockers loafers. He walked right over to the two seats facing my friend and me and sat down. As soon as he was seated, he leaned over to me and spoke to me in perfect English, in a voice full of authority, "Take off your watch and those gold earrings." It was such an extraordinary thing to see a man dressed as he was board the train on the outskirts of Naples, Italy, that I did exactly as he said and took off the watch and earrings. He asked us, "Where are you going?" We told him to Pompeii. He then asked, "Which train stop are you going to use?" We shared with him the stop our hostess had suggested. He immediately told us that was the wrong train stop and that we were to follow him off the train and buy our tickets. He shared with us that we were to use the same train stop as we traveled back to the city later in the day.

We had a couple of train stops left (a ride of approximately 20 minutes), and neither my friend nor I said a word during the remainder of the ride. We just waited to follow him off the train and purchase our tickets. As we left the train, he pointed us to the ticket booth and we went up to buy our tickets for the tour. When we turned to thank him, he was nowhere to be seen. We both looked at one another and said in unison, "That was an angel!" As I have thought of this over the years, I've often wondered why I didn't question him. Where was he from? How would he have known the correct train stop? and so on. We had plenty of time as the train ride continued, but there was something that happened in the atmosphere of that train car when he entered that didn't lend itself to any questioning. Looking back on the day, it was as if the atmosphere and authority of heaven had entered the train car, and we just did as we were told. As I think of that encounter and realize now that my friend and I were in some danger, what strikes me most is the great confidence that day gave me. I now know that if we make the Lord our dwelling, no harm will befall us. For He will command His angels to guard us in all our ways![5]

There are so many wonderful stories like this one when people know angels have visited them.

ANGELIC VISITATION THROUGH THE PORTAL

Angelic visitation is an important concept to understand once the portal of glory has been established connecting heaven and Earth. I have only seen angels a few times, but I do recognize angelic presence. I believe this is a type of discernment that comes through worshiping and knowing the glory of God and how His presence manifests around us. There are really no set rules for angelic appearances. Hebrews 1:14 declares, "Are they not all ministering spirits sent forth to minister for those who will inherit salvation?"

Angels serve both Christ and man. In this section of Hebrews, Jesus is presented as the creator of heaven and Earth and as the immutable one. His superiority is evident in His enthronement. Once we enthrone the Lord, angels are sent to guide, direct and work along with us to accomplish His purpose on Earth. Hebrews 1:13 declares, "But to which of the angels has He ever said: 'Sit at My right hand, till I make Your enemies Your footstool'?" This is a warfare Scripture. We will look at God's order for war and victory in the next chapter.

Notes

1. Dick Eastman, *Heights of Delight* (Ventura, CA: Regal Books, 2002), pp. 52-53.
2. Ernest B. Gentile, *Worship God!* (Portland, OR: City Bible Publishing, 1994), pp. 105-106.
3. Chuck D. Pierce and Rebecca Wagner Sytsema, *Possessing Your Inheritance* (Ventura, CA: Renew Books, 1999), p. 184.
4. Bob Sorge, *Glory: When Heaven Invades the Earth* (Greenwood, MO: Oasis House, 2000), p. 41.
5. Marty Cassady, e-mail to author, March 22, 2002.

THE HOST OF HEAVEN, JUDAH AND THE LION

I am shaking My mane, and getting ready to loose My roar
Lord Sabaoth will lead His people forth
And I am standing at the gate
Standing in judgment at the gate

Against injustice and the strongman of oppression
I roar against covenant breakers and the bloodshed of the innocent
Jezebel and Ahab spirits, false rulers wanting more
Idolatry and poverty shall hear the Lion's roar

I am shaking My mane and getting ready to loose My roar
I am raising the Church up and I am training their hand for war
And I am standing at the gate, making war at the gate

Judah, Judah shall plow
Judah, Judah means praise (to the one true God)
Judah, Judah shall go first
Lawlessness, hear My roar
Unbelief and fear I am telling you, "No more"
Depression, sorrow, grief . . . I am standing at the door
False worship and false religion, I am stirring my zeal for war

I am shaking My mane and getting ready to loose My roar
Who can stand the blast from the presence of the Lord
And I am standing at the gate, taking My stand at the gate

I am shaking My mane, I am shaking My mane
I am shaking My mane
That strong, confident, aggressive Lion in us has been roused and
is shaking His mane and getting ready to loose His roar—in us.
We are His voice.

CHUCK D. PIERCE AND JOHN DICKSON, *JUDAH'S MANE*

The LORD will roar from on high and utter His voice
from His holy habitation; He will roar mightily against
His fold. He will shout like those who tread the grapes,
against all the inhabitants of the earth (Jer. 25:30,
NASB).

THE HEAVENS OPEN

I am disciplined in my pursuit for God. I try to have consistent
time in the Word and worship.

When I was working in downtown Houston, some days I would ride the bus to and from my home in the northern part of the city. I had gotten up one morning and worshiped from 5 A.M to 6 A.M. and was overwhelmed by the presence of God. I then got ready and caught the bus at 7 A.M. On the way to work, I began to read the book of Ephesians. I had just started when I got to Ephesians 1:3-6:

> Blessed be the God and Father of our Lord Jesus Christ, who has blessed us with every spiritual blessing in the heavenly places in Christ, just as He chose us in Him before the foundation of the world, that we should be holy and without blame before Him in love, having predestined us to adoption as sons by Jesus Christ to Himself, according to the good pleasure of His will, to the praise of the glory of His grace, by which He made us accepted in the Beloved.

I began to praise and thank the Lord for choosing me before the foundation of Earth. The heavens opened. I could see all the future blessings that God had for me. I could also see the blessings that were there for the generations before me that were never taken and the blessings that the Lord had for my children to come. Suddenly the Lord began to pour faith into my spirit—it was as if a funnel extended from heaven right into the bus.

I could not contain myself, so I shouted, "Hallelujah!" Those people around me looked startled. I thought to myself, *Surely they can see and feel what I see and feel*. I said, "Lord, I am so filled with faith, I do not know what to do." He said to me: "Give it away to one of those sitting around you." I asked a lady who was sitting in front of me if she had a need and if I could pray for her. She began to share her problems. I knew then what it meant to pray the prayer of faith.

WORSHIP AND ANGELS

Worship and angels go together. All through the Word we find angelic visitation associated with worship. I have seen angels a couple of times. Once when I was a kid, our family was visiting my grandparents who lived on a fairly busy highway in Texas. We were about to cross the road. My younger brother, who was

---

All through the Word we find angelic visitation associated with worship.

---

about 8 at that time, stepped from the ditch to the road first. When he did, I saw a person pull him back into the ditch, and a car pass by at a rapid speed. He lay in the ditch, and all of us, being fearful and astonished, looked for who had pulled him off the road. There was no one. Even as kids, we assumed an angel had intervened.

Another time, I was leading a revival meeting in a town in New Mexico. I saw an angel standing on the left side of the pulpit. I had four ministry teams across the front of the sanctuary. Any time a person would come to the left side of the pulpit, I would see the angel touch him or her. The person would immediately respond to the power that was being released into his or her life. This power would manifest itself in restoration or healing, both physical and spiritual. The people in the meeting all recognized God's supernatural power manifested on the left side of the sanctuary. While I do not always see angels, I do feel angelic presence, especially during worship.

PEOPLE WHO SEE ANGELS

In the last chapter I shared a story from Marty Cassady. She frequently sees angels. When I asked her to tell a little more about how this began, she provided the following:

> To share my story on angels, I must give credit to my daughter, Beth, who is with the Lord now. It was due to an incredible experience she had with an angel that I began to pray that the Lord would allow me to "see" into that Kingdom realm where angels exist.
>
> She was just 23 years old, fresh out of college, working her first job and an active member of a dynamic college and career group at her local church. The leader of this group had a heart for the down and out, and since Beth's heart was also for the lonely, the down and out and the poor, it was natural that she would join in the group's visitations to the inner city to minister. This particular Saturday night they chose the bars of downtown Cincinnati. The plan was that they would just go into the bars, size up the spiritual situation and bless the people as they left a flyer describing their ministry and inviting individuals in the bar to attend. They had visited three bars on that cold November evening and everything had gone according to plan. Many of the bar patrons were unwilling to take a flyer and accept their invitation, but there had been several folks that had expressed an interest. At no point had any in their group felt that there was any danger.
>
> They had only one bar left, and the entrance to that particular establishment had a very narrow door. Whereas the other establishments had doors that allowed one group to enter and another to exit at the

same time, this front door allowed only a single file of people to go in and out. There were five who were ministering that night, and Beth later described the very presence of evil they encountered as they entered the bar. As the members of the team all were feeling the same heaviness, the leader motioned for them just to stand and wait to exit. He had quickly sized up the situation and knew that ministry in this place would be impossible. But there was a rowdy crowd beginning to exit just as they entered. The only thing the group could do was stand and wait for those who were exiting to go through the door before they would be able to leave. As Beth described it, there was such a sense of fear and dread that they knew their safety was at risk. Even knowing the time it would take the group to leave was very short, Beth said she was terrified. She said she squeezed her eyes shut and spoke a prayer asking the Lord to protect them.

Just seconds had passed at this time, and as she opened her eyes she saw a huge angel standing with his back in front of the group of five. He was standing right in front of Beth! She said he was at least 12 feet tall and was so close and so much a part of the "natural" realm she felt that if she had reached out she would have been able to touch him. She described the sense of peace that came over her immediately when she saw this, and the incredible white of his wings, the silver that seemed to be part of the white and the dazzling effect this angelic being had. It was as if looking on this being for more than a few seconds would blind a person. Almost instantly and simultaneously, the leader was motioning for the group to leave as the rowdy crowd had passed through the narrow door and the way was now clear for

the group to leave. As they paused on the sidewalk outside to comment on the fear and dread they had all felt,
the leader of the group asked, "Did you all feel the wave
of peace while we stood there waiting to leave?" And
Beth, asked, "Did you see the angel that came and stood

The Lord showed me that
just as He had spoken to Jeremiah,
He could speak to me.

in front of us?" None had seen the angelic presence
except Beth. It was just a matter of a minute or less, but
the experience left such an impression on her, and her
description of the incident left such an impact on me.

I began to ask the Lord to allow me to "see" as she
had seen. It didn't happen immediately, but I began to
pray that the Lord would allow me to "see," or to ascend
into this Kingdom realm, and the Scripture He led me to
pray was, "Call unto me, and I will answer thee, and
show thee great and mighty things, which thou knowest
not" (Jer. 33:3, *KJV*). I had always thought of this passage
in the context that when I called the Lord would answer
because many versions use the word "tell" in place of
"show." But as I studied the passage I saw that the word
"show" had several meanings: a demonstrative display,
an impressive display or something exhibited especially
for wonder! I also found that it translates "declare,"
"show forth" and finally and most interesting of all,

"messenger." The Lord began to show me that just as He had spoken to Jeremiah when he was confined in the courtyard of the guard (since that was Jeremiah's position when God spoke this Scripture to him), He could speak to me in the "confines" of the natural and "show" me those great and mighty things that I had not known that exist in the spiritual realm as we ascend. I began to pray in earnest that the Lord would allow me to see an angel.[1]

There are not set rules for angelic appearances. The one thing we do know is that God's Word declares that angels are ministering spirits to serve those who will inherit salvation (see Heb. 1:14). We also know that ministering spirits transcend to the natural realm from the spiritual realm. As we ascend in worship, we also know that a portal opens for angelic visitation. During our times of prayer and crying out to God, during those times when we worship with abandonment as David did, we enter the realm of the spirit. Psalm 37:4 shows us that as we delight ourselves in the Lord he gives us the desires of our heart.

Marty had more to say about when she ascends in worship:

There are many times I get just a peek into that heavenly realm, and often it includes angel sightings. But just as often I'll be going about my business as usual and catch a glimpse of angels. Just last week, as I returned from a trip to Florida flying through Chicago, I looked down from the plane and saw a host of angels over the city of Chicago. I knew their presence was an answer to someone's prayer or ascension experience to protect the city and begin to bring revival. In November 2001, as I was before the Lord, I had a vision of the heavenlies. The Lord allowed me to see thousands upon thousands, even ten thousands upon ten thousands of angels. They stood, with swords in their hands, ready to be dispatched at the word of the Lord. And I heard the Spirit of the Lord say, "These are the thousands that have been reserved for the end times. Call to me when you need their release and remember that as you see these, there are far more that are for you than the number of those against you."[2]

In *Angels: God's Secret Agents*, Billy Graham writes:

The Bible states that angels, like men, were created by God. At one time no angels existed; indeed there was nothing but the Triune God: Father, Son and Holy Spirit. Paul, in Colossians 1:16 says, "For by Him were all things created, that are in heaven, and that are in earth, visible and invisible." Angels indeed are among the invisible things made by God, for "all things were created by him, and for him." This Creator, Jesus, "is before all things, and by him all things consist" (Col. 1:17), so that even angels would cease to exist if Jesus, who is Almighty God, did not sustain them by His power.

It seems that angels have the ability to change their appearance and shuttle in a flash from the capital glory of heaven to earth and back again. Although some interpreters have said that the phrase "sons of God" in Genesis 6:2 refers to angels, the Bible frequently makes it clear that angels are non-material; Hebrews 1:14 calls them ministering "spirits." Intrinsically, they don't possess physical bodies, although they may take on physical bodies when God appoints them to special tasks. Further, God has given them no ability to reproduce, and they neither marry nor are given in marriage (Mark

12:25). The empire of angels is as vast as God's creation. If you believe the Bible, you will believe in their ministry. They crisscross the Old and New Testaments, being mentioned directly or indirectly nearly three hundred times.[3]

ANGELS: WHO ARE THEY?

An angel is a heavenly messenger who delivers a message to humans, carries out God's will, praises God or guards God's Throne. The term "angel" is derived from the Greek word *angelo*, which means "messenger." The Hebrew equivalent, *malak*, also means "messenger." The task of angels is to convey the message or do the will of God who sent them. Effective intercessors, individuals who "stand in the gap," understand angelic help because they are called to mediate through prayer.

Other terms applied to angels include "sons of God," "holy ones" and "heavenly host." These are celestial beings who worship God, attend God's Throne or comprise God's army. These "hosts" colabor with the grandeur, power or acts of God.

Winged angels are another category of heavenly beings. We find cherubim and seraphim appearing in the visions of Isaiah (see Isa. 6:2-6) and Ezekiel (see Ezek. 1:4-28; 10:3-22). Cherubim guard or attend the divine Throne. Seraphim attend God's Throne and also voice praises. Angels seem to have order and a fixed rank system (see 1 Thess. 4:16; Jude 9).

There are varied appearances of angels throughout the Word of God. Many times in the Old Testament angels appear as ordinary men. However, other times they clearly come as non human. In the New Testament they can have a brilliant white appearance.

Angels are created beings, and are responsible for guarding God's purposes on Earth. Matthew 18:10 quotes Jesus: "Take heed that do you not despise one of these little ones, for I say to you that in heaven their angels always see the face of My Father who is in heaven." This clearly shows us that individuals have protective angels. Angels also guard specific churches (see Dan. 10:13; Acts 12:15; Rev. 1:20; 2—3).

Angels are called princes over nations. We find this example in Daniel concerning Michael. Some of the basic tasks of angels include announcing, proclaiming, protecting and punishing. In a later chapter I will examine how angels relate to us on Earth through worship and war.

LORD SABAOTH: THE LORD OF HOSTS

One of the names and characteristics of God is Lord Sabaoth. The Hebrew word *tsebha'oth* means hosts or armies. We also find references to Lord Sabaoth in the New Testament in Romans 9:29, where the author refers to the book of Isaiah and declares, "Unless the LORD of Sabaoth had left us a seed, we would have become like Sodom, and we would have been made like Gomorrah." God in His mercy secures a remnant through the working of the host of heaven. He does this to keep apostasy from reigning on Earth. We see in context that Lord Sabaoth is the almighty God who leads the hosts of heaven. The Lord Sabaoth is the:

1. God of the armies of Earth;
2. God of the armies of the stars;
3. God of the unseen armies of angels.

When we worship, He begins to order and align His armies for victory. "Hosts" signifies an organized group under authority. God has a multitude of ready and able servants. This suggests that the Lord is the commander and chief of the armies in heaven.

The most prevalent use of this name of God is found in Zechariah. When it was time to rebuild the Temple, God intervened as Lord Sabaoth. Zechariah 4:6 is a wonderful Scripture: "Not by might nor by power, but by My Spirit, says the LORD of Hosts." This verse shows how Lord Sabaoth works. He releases strength, power, force, valor, substance and wealth. He organizes an army that is available to build our future. The Lord of Hosts comes to remove any obstacle that has been placed in our paths.

One timeless hymn that acknowledges this character of God is "A Mighty Fortress Is Our God." Based on Psalm 46, this song was written by Martin Luther.

> A mighty fortress is our God, a bulwark never failing;
> Our helper He amid the flood of mortal ills prevailing.
> For still our ancient foe doth seek to work us woe—
> His craft and power are great, and, armed with cruel
>   hate,
> On earth is not His equal.
>
> Did we in our own strength confide, our striving would
>   be losing,
> Were not the right man on our side, the man of God's
>   own choosing.
> Dost ask who that may be? Christ Jesus, it is He—
> Lord Sabaoth His name, from age to age the same,
> And He must win the battle.
>
> And though this world with devils filled, should threat-
>   en to undo us,
> We will not fear, for God hath willed His truth to tri-
>   umph through us.
> The prince of darkness grim, we tremble not for him—

His rage we can endure, for lo, his doom is sure:
One little word shall fell him.

That word above all earthly powers, no thanks to them,
    abideth;
The Spirit and the gifts are ours through Him who
    with us sideth.
Let goods and kindred go, this mortal life also—
The body they may kill; God's truth abideth still:
His kingdom is forever.[4]

THE SOUND OF RESTORATION

God's sound permeates from heaven and orders much of what
goes on in the earthly realm. When He is ready to bring restoration to Earth, He releases His sound.

> God's sound permeates from heaven and orders much of what goes on in the earthly realm.

Physical sound is created when something vibrates. Sometimes we can see the vibration, and sometimes we cannot. When we clap our hands or stomp our feet, vibration occurs. This causes air to move. The source of the sound vibrates and pushes the molecules through the air and into our ears, and our brains then interpret it as sound.

Sound, when unorganized, produces noise. Sound, when organized, produces music. When an instrument is blown by a person, the air inside resonates. How an instrument sounds depends upon how fast the air vibrates, and this depends on the length of the column of air inside the instrument. Short vibrations produce high notes; long vibrations produce low notes. The regularity of the vibrations of air produces music as opposed to noise.

Music played an important part in Hebraic culture. Jubal, the son of Lamech, "was the father of all those who play the harp and flute" (Gen. 4:21). The close relationship between the pasture, the field and the musical arts is shown in that Jubal had an elder brother, Jabal, who was "father of those who dwell in tents and have livestock" (Gen. 4:20). Music was used at most key occasions in the Bible. Laban reproached Jacob for stealing away without allowing him to cheer his departure "with joy and songs, with timbrel and harp" (Gen. 31:27).

THE SOUND OF MUSIC

There were songs of triumph after victory in battle (see Exod. 15:1; Judg. 5:1). Miriam and the women celebrated the downfall of Pharaoh and his horsemen "with timbrels and with dances" (Exod. 15:20), and Jehoshaphat returned victorious to Jerusalem "with stringed instruments and harps and trumpets" (2 Chron. 20:28). Music, singing and dancing were common at feasts (see Isa. 5:12; Amos 6:5). In particular, they were features of the vintage festivals (see Isa. 16:10) and of marriage celebrations. Kings had singers and instrumentalists (see 2 Sam. 19:35; Eccles. 2:8). The shepherd boy had his lyre (see 1 Sam. 16:18). The young men at the gates enjoyed their music (see Lam. 5:14).

Music was used at times of mourning. . . . The dirge that constitutes the book of Lamentations and David's lament over Saul and Jonathan (see 2 Sam. 1:18-27) are notable examples. It became the custom to hire professional mourners to assist at funerals. These regularly included flutists (see Matt. 9:23). Even the harlot increased her seductive powers with song (see Isa. 23:16).[5]

SOUND IN THE AIR

Air is so transparent that we can easily forget about it. Yet it is real and substantial. Without air, life on Earth would be impossible. Air not only provides the oxygen that humans and all other animals need to breathe; it is also a major part of our environment. The atmosphere of air surrounding our planet protects us from the harmful effects of cosmic rays and meteors, and, like a fluffy comforter, keeps the Earth's surface warm. . . . Enveloping the world is a thick blanket of gases called the atmosphere. Without this blanket to protect us, we would be roasted by the Sun during the day, then frozen at night as all its heat escaped into space. The outer reaches of the atmosphere are many hundreds of miles above us. But most of the gases are squeezed into the lowest nine miles or so.[6]

We have already seen that when sound comes into air, the air changes. When God releases His voice, creation must respond. When we serve as God's voice on Earth, Earth responds to the sound we release. Psalm 29 declares,

Give unto the LORD, O you mighty ones, give unto the LORD glory and strength. Give unto the LORD the glory due to His name; worship the LORD in the beauty of holiness.

The voice of the LORD is over the waters; the God of glory thunders; the LORD is over many waters. The voice of the LORD is powerful; the voice of the LORD is full of majesty. The voice of the LORD breaks the cedars, yes, the LORD splinters the cedars of Lebanon. He makes them also skip like a calf, Lebanon and Sirion like a young wild ox. The voice of the LORD divides the flames of fire. The voice of the LORD shakes the wilderness; the LORD shakes the Wilderness of Kadesh. The voice of the LORD makes the deer give birth, and strips the forests bare; and in His temple everyone says, "Glory!" The LORD sat enthroned at the Flood, and the LORD sits as King forever. The LORD will give strength to His people; the LORD will bless His people with peace.

When we express ourselves in worship to the Lord, the air vibrates with our worship. This causes our environment to change. In his book *Worship God!,* Ernest Gentile shares various worship forms of the Psalms:

> When we release a sound of worship, the earth must respond. There is power in lifting our *voices* in acclamation of the true and living God. We can speak; we can sing; we can shout. Then the expressive power of the *hands* generates a sound. We can clap, and we can play instruments. We can also lift our hands in worship. Additionally, there is a posture of worship. We can stand; we can bow; we can dance.[7]

MUSIC, REVIVAL AND AWAKENING

Music has always been a natural by-product of revival. In David's great revival of 1000 B.C., music exploded in the tent he pitched to house the Ark of the Covenant. New instruments had to be invented to facilitate the new worship coming forth. The birth of the Church brought a resurgence of music as God began to restore David's fallen tent. Accounts of the Early Church depicted lively times of praise and worship.

Christ-filled hearts have always found a way of expression in psalms, hymns and spiritual songs. We have records of hymns by Church fathers such as Ambrose, the bishop of Milan and Augustine of Hippo, who used hymns to direct people's hearts to God and to reinforce sound doctrine, which was being eroded by the Roman government.[8]

Christ-filled hearts have always found a way of expression in psalms, hymns and spiritual songs.

In the sixth and seventh centuries, Gregory the Great (540-604) collected and compiled hymns and chants for use throughout the Church that became known as the Gregorian chants.[9] In the eighth century, Charlemagne wanted these chants to be sung in his kingdom (the Holy Roman Empire). No method of Western musical notation was yet in use, so over time rhythmic details were added to the chants to help in their spread, and then pitch-defined manuscripts begin to appear. By the eleventh century complete written repertories of the chant with music were developed.[10]

As the Protestant Reformation unfolded in the fifteenth and sixteenth centuries and beyond, fresh new hymns sprang up in their new churches, replacing Gregorian chants. First the Moravians then the Lutherans used hymns to express their hearts toward God.

Martin Luther wrote and gathered hymns that captured the life of this revival. Some of the melodies used were original; others were borrowed from familiar secular songs or derived from

Gregorian chants themselves. The lyrics, like those of earlier Church fathers reinforced the doctrines of the faith and inspired Christian hearts. So on through the next centuries, hymn writers captured the fire of each new revival as it sprang into blaze. In the eighteenth century, William Williams, considered the poet laureate of the Welsh revival, was inspired by the fiery preaching of Howell Harris. Williams joined the ranks of revival preachers and produced 800 Welsh hymns. Soon after, in America, the Great Awakening burst on the scene under the preaching of John Wesley. His brother, Charles, eclipsed all other hymn writers, penning an amazing 6,500 hymns.

On through the nineteenth century and into the twentieth, hymns played their part in the revivals that propelled the church forward: from the Second Great Awakening to the Pentecostal revival to the Latter Rain movement. In America and other places, hymn writers began to depart from the "high church" sound that Europe had drawn from the somber majesty of the Gregorian chants. Many hymns began to take on the "folk sound" of the common people and later the "gospel sound" of the twentieth century.

The biggest change in the music of the Church since the Reformation came in the 1960s with the charismatic movement. People began to sing simple choruses and Scripture songs along with the hymns and eventually in their place. Through the subsequent renewal movements of the 1970s, 1980s and 1990s, these simple songs developed in style and content, encompassing a variety of sounds and styles, both secular and uniquely Christian. The technology of the information age facilitated the swift spread of innumerable songs to congregations around the planet. Christian Copyright Licensing International has cataloged 60,000 Christian songs presently in circulation. But even this does not take into account countless thousands of songs congregations have used that have been created by their own members.

With this resurgence of creative worship that typified David's Tabernacle, we have exploded into the new millennium equipped with the keys of David to ascend through the strata into the heavens to obtain the strategies necessary to possess all the nations called by His name (see Amos 9). We saw a renewal sound come during the 1980s and 1990s. Then, of course, a prophetic sound entered into the renewal sound, which pointed the Church into a new place. We have now entered into a season of war. From a position of intimacy I believe we will gain the sound that will cause victory on Earth.

GOD HAS AN ORDER FOR VICTORY

As music formed an integral part of Hebraic social life, so it had its place in their religious life. First Chronicles 15:16-24 contains a detailed account of the organization by David of the Levitical choir and orchestra. Apart from this passage there are only scattered and indirect references to the use of music in religious worship; however, we have enough biblical evidence to form a clear impression of the character of the musical service of the Temple. Although we have no evidence regarding the instrumental music of the Temple, we can discover from the form of the Psalms that they were intended to be sung antiphonally either by two choirs (see Pss. 13; 20; 38) or by a choir and the congregation (see Pss. 136; 118:1-4). It appears that after the captivity the choirs were formed of an equal number of male and female voices (see Ezra 2:65).

The first place we find God began to mobilize His troops to move forward into their inheritance was Exodus 6:26, which declares, "Bring out the children of Israel from the land of Egypt according to their armies [hosts]." To do that, He had an order. Moses' tabernacle, which was a shadow of things to come, was surrounded by the tribes and their armies. The tribes on the east and south set out first. Judah was the lead tribe (see Num. 2).

JUDAH LEADS

There is a great inheritance that He has for each one of us individually. He also has a corporate inheritance that He is calling the Body of Christ into that will affect each territory throughout the nations of the earth. The time is NOW to war for our inheritance. There are personal promises God wants to manifest. This

> This is a time of the preparation and shifting of the mantle of authority for the next generation.

is a time of the preparation and shifting of the mantle of authority for the next generation. How do we proceed?

Look at how Judges 1:1-2 relates:

> Now after the death of Joshua it came to pass that the children of Israel asked the LORD, saying, "Who shall be first to go up for us against the Canaanites to fight against them?" And the LORD said, "Judah shall go up. Indeed, I have delivered the land into his hand."

Judah was selected as the tribe of divine preeminence in Jacob's patriarchal blessing.

Genesis 49:8-10 gives us more insight:

Judah, you are he whom your brothers shall praise; your hand shall be on the neck of your enemies; your father's children shall bow down before you. Judah is a lion's whelp; from the prey, my son, you have gone up. He bows down, he lies down as a lion; and as a lion, who shall rouse him? The scepter shall not depart from Judah, nor a lawgiver from between his feet, until Shiloh comes; and to Him shall be the obedience of the people.

Judah must go first. Praise must take its preeminence within our lives, churches, cities, states and nation. When Judah goes first, the scepter of authority is then in place for ultimate victory. This is a time that the Lion of Judah will roar louder than the lion that has sought to devour us!

JUDAH MEANS PRAISE

Judah means praise Yahweh. In this season, a major shift is coming in the way we worship and acknowledge God corporately. The word "praise" originates from "value" and "price." Yahweh signifies the God of covenant. This is a time when God values our worship. Also, this is a time when we begin to value the covenant that He has allowed us to enter into with Him. What a price He paid to give us access to the throne room. Our worship will take on great covenant significance in this time. Our worship will release great blessings into the earthly realm. The redeemed of the Lord will say so. This is a time when the burning bush, "I AM," type of worship is coming into the midst of God's people. This is going to release a deliverance call across Earth.

Deliverers will rise up! Entire groups of people will begin to be delivered from the bondage and oppression that has kept them prostrate, and they will begin to stand before the Lord with great shouts of victory. This is a time of much confrontation. But when the confrontation of the enemy comes from intimate communion and worship, we are assured victory. This is a time when we must give Judah (our praise and worship) the freedom to experiment until we come into the sound that will bring victory into the earthly realm. We must distinguish the sound of Judah. "The LORD also will *roar* from Zion . . . the heavens and earth will shake . . . the LORD will be a shelter for His people, and the strength of the children of Israel" (Joel 3:16, emphasis added). God roars as He goes to battle. He will roar against His covenant enemies. His covenant people will also begin to roar and become a fearful, holy remnant to contend with in the earthly realm. He will be a shelter and a strength to those who respond to His sound and call on Him. Worship this season will determine how the multitudes in the valley of decision begin to decide to follow God. There is an inherited roar within you. Let the Lord draw you near and develop that roar within you so that this sound is brought forth at the appropriate time in your life this season.

TIME TO GO FORTH IN PRAISE

Worship causes us to move thankfully with our body toward our creator. Praise (or *yadah*) is to worship God with extended hands. With hands lifted up, we declare the merit of God, and we thank Him for everything He has put in our hands. We find this concept first mentioned in the Bible when Leah conceived her fourth son and named him Judah, meaning praise. When Jacob acknowledged Judah, he extended his highest blessing upon him and declared that even his brothers would praise him. He also declared that Judah (praise) would triumph over all of his enemies with royal authority (the scepter) and legal authority (the lawgiver). The word "Judah" also means to hold out your hand

and throw or shoot a stone or an arrow at your enemy. Therefore, we find that praise will be a key weapon of the Spirit of God in our lives in days ahead.

Praise is a response to God's revelation of Himself that every child of God should express. Human praise of a holy God is a major theme throughout God's Word. Praise is expressing to God our appreciation and understanding of His worth. Praise says "thank-you" for each aspect of God's nature. Praise expands our awareness of God's character. "Praise" comes from a Latin word meaning "value" or "prize." When we praise God, we proclaim His merit or worth and His value to us here on Earth. We find other words related to praise in the Bible, including "glory," "blessing," "thanksgiving" and "hallelujah." During this season, these are all words that I love to express over you. I like the order of the Lord's Prayer in Luke 11:2 "Father . . . hallowed be Your name. Your kingdom come." First, Jesus praised God. Then He made His request. Praising God puts us in the right frame of mind to begin to declare our needs to a holy Father. With our hands outstretched we can worship God in such a way that our daily provision can be released. Through worship we can be assured that our supply will always come to us in a timely manner. Praise and thanksgiving are the opposite of worry. One of our greatest worries is over our needs being met. This is a time to be thankful for all that God is doing in our lives. Be like the one leper who went back and thanked Jesus for his healing. This thankfulness produced not just healing, but wholeness. Be whole!

There is also a price to pay to enter into praise and worship. There is a cost to this process, and we are faced with a fundamental issue: Will we choose to enjoy the efforts of others, or will we enter into the sacrifice of praise? Furthermore, will we choose to offer this sacrifice in the good times as well as the trials? In *The Power of Praise and Worship*, Terry Law writes:

God is not interested only in the praise that we give Him in times when things are going well. He is after that praise that comes in the midst of great trial, great difficulty, grief, sickness, demonic oppression, temptation, relational difficulties, and financial problems. He still requires praise. He still demands it. When we give it to Him in time of difficulty it means all the more to Him. *We are operating according to the principle of sacrifice, and God is pleased.*[11]

THE PATHWAY TO GOD'S PRESENCE

Judah led the tribe of Israel through the wilderness. Numbers 2:3 reads, "On the east side, toward the rising of the sun, those of the standard of the forces with Judah shall camp according to their armies." Judah also led the conquest of Canaan. Therefore, it will be praise that leads us forth into our battles and victories ahead.

Praise causes the presence of the Lord to come into our midst.

Praise causes the presence of the Lord to come into our midst. Even though God is omniscient, He manifests His authority and rule in our environment when we praise Him. *When we praise, God comes in and leads us forth.* The word "inhabit" or "enthrone" means to settle in or marry. When we praise and worship, we restore our communion with a holy God. We become one! He does not just visit us, but He abides and aligns

Himself with us to walk with us into the path that He has chosen for us. He partners with us like a spouse. When we praise,
our faith and trust increases. The word "inhabit" or "enthrone"
(*yashab*) also means to judge in ambush. Therefore, He seats
Himself in the very middle of our lives and judges the enemies
that surround us. Just think of God seated in the very center of
your life. No enemy is able to dethrone you because He cannot
be overcome. That's worship!

BEING LED TO THE
WAR AHEAD

Knowing that we are entering a battle of uncharted terrain, worship and praise seems to be our key to victory in days ahead. We
have now entered the season of war. When we began this last
millennium, change and conflict accelerated. We find ourselves
groping for stability, footing and positioning. The world is
changing so quickly that many awaken with anxiety to each new
day. Societal institutions are shifting at such a pace that from
region to region the entire earth seems to be in a constant state
of earthquake.

A word synonymous with conflict is "warfare." In warfare we
must clash with an enemy, whether of a tangible nature or a discerned perception. During this time in history, I think I find
much comfort in Ecclesiastes 3:1,8: "To everything there is a season, a time for every purpose under heaven . . . a time of war!"
When it is a time for war, we must have a paradigm for war! We
are experiencing a time in our nation when we are entering into
a new war. However, this war is not just physical but spiritual.
The Church is being prepared to enter its most dynamic season
of warfare, worship and harvest. We will examine this more fully
later in this book. The real issue is that without His presence, we
are destined for defeat.

The apostle Paul tells us that these accounts of Israel's journey to the Promised Land were given to us as an example (see 1 Cor. 10:1-11). God is demonstrating something to us in the order of procession of the tribes. You or I might think that Ruben should have gone first: He was the oldest, and with age comes wisdom and experience. But this was not God's decisive factor. Joseph was the favorite, as well as the most successful and powerful of his brothers, but this was not God's criterion. The example God wanted to give us was that praise should always lead the way.

Leah, as we all know, was unloved. It was Rachel whom Jacob had wanted and had worked for. But Jacob was tricked into taking Leah instead. Not a good start for a relationship; but she tried hard as she could to gain Jacob's affection. In those days, a high value was put on a woman who could produce children. God caused Leah to be fruitful, and she bore Jacob three sons, each time hoping to procure her husband's love because of them, but to no avail. Finally she turned her heart toward the Lord. "She conceived again and bore a son and said, 'This time I will praise the LORD.' Therefore she named him Judah" (Gen. 29:35, *NASB*).

So the name Judah comes to us as a true representation of what praise should be: worshiping with extended hands toward God in the midst of any kind of circumstance. Leah could have succumbed to her rejection and named her son "bitter" or "unfulfilled," but her heart was set now on God, not man. She chose to praise God rather than nurse her self-pity. Judah was the last child Leah would bear, and his name would always be before her to remind her of her decision. It is this kind of praise that God sends first, not praise that is dependent on the circumstances, because the circumstances might not always be favorable. But the praise going forth first must always be unshakable.

God gives us strategies that are not of the wisdom of this world. The example He has presented to us is to send Judah first, not necessarily the wisest or the strongest. Let praise lead the way. Praise breaks through. Jehoshaphat was able to win the day by sending his praise team first (see 2 Chron. 20:20-22).

Unshakable praise plows through the hardest ground. God says in Hosea 10:11, "Judah will plow." When the ground is hard, when the circumstances are adverse, God's favor is on the one who will lead off with praise. Fallow ground will break up. The plow of praise will cut through ungiving Earth and make a way for the good seed of the Word to be planted.

Later, as recorded in Judges, Israel was up against a different kind of challenge. It was an enemy within. One of their own tribes, Benjamin, harbored a homosexual gang guilty of rape and murder (see Judg. 19:16-30). The other tribes gathered and asked for the lawless men to be given up for punishment, but Benjamin stood by them. "Now the sons of Israel arose, went up to Bethel, and inquired of God and said, 'Who shall go up first for us to battle against the sons of Benjamin?' Then the LORD said, 'Judah shall go up first' " (Judg. 20:18, *NASB*).

So Judah is again required to lead the way, but this time it comes at a staggering cost. Israel is beaten back and loses many warriors. The next day God tells Israel to go again, and again they suffer much and are driven back. But here is where unshakable praise does not give up. "Come, let us return to the LORD. For He has torn us, but He will heal us; He has wounded us, but He will bandage us. He will revive us after two days; He will raise us up on the third day, that we may live before Him" (Hos. 6:1-2, *NASB*).

There is power for God's people on the third day, for that is the day of resurrection power. Though Israel had been obedient, they had been torn and wounded in those first two days. Here is where we often give up, just one day before resurrection. Psalm

30:5 reads, "Weeping may last for the night, but a shout of joy comes in the morning" (*NASB*). Unshakable praise must keep going. On the third day, Israel inquired of God and He said to go again. They did and God delivered Benjamin into their hands. The power of sin that had ensnared and deceived Benjamin was broken, and they were able to be restored.

Judah goes first through wilderness experiences. Judah goes first in the war for our inheritance. Judah goes first to plow a way into new territory. Judah goes first when the cost is great.

A New Song: The Lion of Judah Will Roar

At a conference, Barbara Wentroble was teaching on how Satan roams about like a roaring lion, seeking whom he may devour, but that we had the Lion of Judah in us. John Dickson says:

> God dropped a song in my spirit as she spoke, and when she finished, she looked at me and asked, "John, do you have a song?" I said yes, and sang the song God had given me:
>
> **RAISE UP A ROAR**
>
> When that ol' lion roars against me, my God rises in me
> 'Cause He has a roar of His own
> I know the Lion of Judah is the King of the Jungle
> —And He roars from His throne
> Raise up a roar, raise up a roar
> Raise up a roar, the King is on His throne
> Greater is He that is in me than He that is in the
> world[12]

Revelation 5:5 tells us that Jesus is the Lion of Judah. That lion is living in us. Satan only roams about "like" a roaring lion. Jesus *is* a roaring lion. We have to let that aspect of praise be in us. That lion in us is strong, confident, aggressive and not to be roused. "They will walk after the LORD, He will roar like a lion;

There is a sound of God being released in the earth right now through His people.

---

indeed He will roar" (Hos. 11:10, *NASB*). There is a sound of God being released in the earth right now through His people that is signifying the strength of God in these times. The enemy is walking around like a roaring lion seeking whom he will devour, sounding accusations and producing fear. God is releasing His roar, which is much greater than the enemy's. We will discuss later how the new song breaks the old cycle and breaks demonic hosts.

UNTIL SHILOH COMES

Judah is to lead until Shiloh comes (see Gen. 49:10). Shiloh was a city where the tabernacle was set up (see Josh. 18:1). Here in Genesis it appears to be a proper name or a messianic designation of Jesus. One idea is that *shiloh* means "the peaceful one." Another view is that shiloh is a noun with a pronominal suffix that should be understood to mean "his son"; thus, lawgivers and princes would not depart from Judah until his son comes. Another possibility is to divide shiloh into the two words *shay* and *loh*, which would mean "the one to whom tribute is brought." The most likely meaning of shiloh is the one accepted by most of the ancient Jewish authorities who understood shiloh to be a word compounded from *shel* and *loh*, meaning "to whom it belongs." *Shelloh* may be expressed by the English phrases: "to whom dominion belongs," "whose is the kingdom" and "he whose right it is to reign."

Samuel's early years provided another connection with Shiloh (see 1 Sam. 1—4). At the tabernacle, Hannah vowed to the Lord that if He would give her a son she would give him back to God (see 1 Sam. 1). After the birth of Samuel, Hannah brought him to Shiloh in gratitude to God (see 1 Sam. 1:24-28). Thus, Shiloh became home for Samuel as he lived under the care of Eli, the high priest, and his two wicked sons, Hophni and Phinehas. Samuel was the first transitional prophet whom we find during the change of government and form of worship in the Word of God. Later, Samuel received the Lord's message that the priest-hood would be taken from Eli's family (see 1 Sam. 3). Years later, following a defeat at Aphek, the Israelite army sent for the Ark of the Covenant from Shiloh. Mistakenly thinking that the Ark would bring victory, the Israelites lost the second battle of Aphek to the Philistines. Results included losing the Ark; the deaths of Hophni, Phinehas and Eli; and the apparent conquering of Shiloh (see 1 Sam. 4). So in other words, Judah will continue to lead until dominion belongs to the rightful King of the kingdom.

THE SOUND OF THE THRONE ROOM

A physical sound has always led the armies of God forth. I always visualize it this way: God is on His Throne, and Jesus is seated next to Him. Jesus is the door that we have into the Father's Throne. The Word of God tells us in James 5 to submit ourselves to God, draw near to Him and then resist the devil. I believe that as we worship and submit ourselves to a holy God, we can come into intimate contact with Him. Even though we walk here on the earth in our worshipful submission, we ascend into heaven. As we individually seek God and ascend into the Throne Room, we can hear the sound in heaven in our spirit man on Earth.

God always led His people forth with sound. We find in Numbers 10 that trumpets would sound. We also find this all the way through the book of Revelation. The book of Revelation is just an incredible, elaborate pageant that is interpreted to us by heavenly, celestial singers along with creatures and elders. John saw a door standing open in heaven, and the voice he heard was like a trumpet speaking and saying, "Come up here and I will show you things that must take place after this" (see Rev. 1:10). The Lord's voice many times sounds like a trumpet calling us forth. The trumpet, or shofar, in the Word of God had a distinct sound to assemble and call God's people to war. Another sound we find before God led His troops forward was "the wind in the mulberry trees." In 2 Samuel 5, David had experienced a major breakthrough in his own life. What had been prophesied over him 29 years prior had actually come into fulfillment. He then had to lead the armies forth into battle. David had one driving purpose: to get the Ark of the Covenant of God back into its rightful position in the midst of God's covenant people. When the Philistines heard that David had been anointed as king, they rose up against him. David defeated and drove them back out of his jurisdictional authority. However, they regrouped and started coming back at him again. He then asked the Lord if he was to pursue them. In 2 Samuel 5:24 the Lord answers, "And . . . when you hear the sound of the marching in the tops of the mulberry trees, then you shall advance quickly." The sound of marching is not just the wind blowing the tops of the trees, but it is the hosts of heaven and the armies of God rustling the leaves and signifying they were present to help David in victory. In the book of Revelation, we find the real issue is relationship between the sounds of heaven and the demonstration of God on Earth. Sound leads us forth.

HOW TO LEAD ASCENDING WORSHIP

There are many aspects of worship. All of these come into play when we come together as the Church. Corporate worship takes on a broader dimension than any individual's lifestyle of worship. Several dynamics change when we come together as the Church:

1. **An increase of strength.** One can put 1,000 to flight, but two can put 10,000 to flight (see Deut. 32:30). This is a valuable principle of multiplication.

2. **The power of agreement.** Jesus told us, "Again I say to you, that if two of you agree on earth about anything that they may ask, it shall be done for them by My Father who is in heaven" (Matt. 18:19, *NASB*). This is the power of agreement that increases the effectiveness of our prayers. The word "agree" means to come into harmony with. It actually means we make the same sound on Earth that is coming from heaven. Therefore, our sounds are in harmony.

3. **The Lord's presence.** We have a special promise from Jesus that He, Himself, will show up when we gather together in His name. "For where two or three have gathered together in My name, I am there in their midst" (Matt. 18:20, *NASB*). When we come together, He is there with us.

4. **The corporate Body of Christ.** One of the greatest mysteries is that we become something beyond what

we are as individuals when we assemble. We become the Body of Christ. He is the head, we are the body. This determines the expression of our worship. What the head is thinking the Body should respond to accordingly. "Now you are Christ's body, and individually members of it" (1 Cor. 12:27, *NASB*). In this passage, Paul is explaining how each of us has a different spiritual gift, a different aspect of Christ's ministry that when brought together make up His fullness in one corporate Body. "But the manifestation of the Spirit is given . . . for the profit of all" (1 Cor. 12:7). The human body is a complex organism. It has a synergistic quality of many parts all working together to produce a whole expression. Each member of the body is dependent on other members of the body. Each also contributes to the best of others. Just think what would happen if we came together in a place of worship where we all responded fully to the head. How glorious. "For even as the body is one and yet has many members, and all the members of the body, though they are many, are one body, so also is Christ" (1 Cor. 12:12, *NASB*). "But now God has placed the members, each one of them, in the body, just as He desired" (1 Cor. 12:18, *NASB*). When we are obeying and expressing ourself the way the head would have us express ourself, we create an individual symphony of worship.

A SUBMITTED ORDER
FOR WORSHIP

David presents a great example of submission to God and its relationship to worship. The order of worship under David's reign also presents a great example of how corporate worship is ordered and submitted. The worship team submitted to the worship leaders. Therefore, David's anointing would flow through the worship leaders into the worship team. David's worship leaders submitted themselves to David. And because of that, they came up under the anointing that was in David. The sons of David's three worship leaders, Asaph, Heman and Ethan (Jeduthun), were appointed to prophesy in the Tabernacle. In corporate worship, they were unable to just worship at their own discretion. They were being trained and given direction in their prophesying, "the sons of Asaph were under the direction of Asaph, who prophesied under the direction of the king" (1 Chron. 25:2, *NASB*).

The Word goes on to say the same thing about the other two worship leaders and their sons. The sons prophesied under the direction of their fathers, the worship leaders, who prophesied under the direction of David, the king. As they came under the authority of the one over them, they had faith to step out in their gift and know they would be backed up by the one over them in the chain of command. Being under authority did not hinder them; it enabled them.

Jesus taught the same thing about His relationship with the Father. He did nothing except as He first saw the Father doing it (see John 5:18). I define this as *true worship*. Therefore, when you read about the life of Jesus, you can see He was teaching us how to worship and respond in humility to a holy God. In his book *Humility*, Peter Wagner writes,

> "Whoever exalts himself will be humbled, and whoever humbles himself will be exalted" (Matt. 23:12, *NIV*). In this short Scripture passage we find two parallel pairs of active and passive verbs. By *active* verbs, I mean that we must *choose* to initiate. If we do not decide to do this certain thing, it simply will not happen, regardless of what we may

know theologically to be God's perfect will. That is so important that I will be coming back to this thought again and again. In other words, it basically depends on us! On the other hand, the *passive* verb does not depend on us at all. If we decide, rightly or wrongly, to do the active verb, the passive thing will inevitably happen to us whether we want it to or not. We might say that the active takes *human* initiative, while the passive takes *divine* initiative.[13]

THE ROLE OF PROPHETIC SINGING

In 2 Chronicles 20, we find that worship was the order and the key of victory. We also find that prophetic release was very important to have the strategy to win in the battle. Worship and war are key elements for us to understand for our ultimate victory. In this story, a number of Judah's enemies came together

> Worship and war are key elements for us to understand for our ultimate victory.

to form a confederation against Judah and were planning to invade Judah's God-ordained, God-promised boundaries. In obedience to the Lord, Judah had not previously invaded those who were in the confederation and who were now arising to steal what rightfully belonged to Judah. There was no question that the combined strength of the enemies could easily have overthrown Judah.

Jehoshaphat, who was a godly king, cried out to the Lord for a strategy for the warfare his people faced. As he addressed the people he said, "Believe in the LORD your God, and you shall be established; believe His prophets, and you shall prosper" (2 Chron. 20:20). In *The Best Is Yet Ahead*, Becky Wagner Sytsema and I wrote the process for victory that gained Judah the strategy to overcome the enemy: The people of Judah fasted. They inquired of the Lord. They reminded God of His promises. They became utterly dependent on the Lord as their help. They got in the proper position to face the enemy (our abiding place). They sought counsel. Then they worshiped and praised the Lord. We elaborate on this last point:

> There is, perhaps, no stronger weapon of warfare than praise and worship to the Lord. Satan hates our worship to God for many reasons. For one, he is jealous of our worship. He longs to obtain it for himself through whatever means he can. For another, he knows that the weapon of worship is strong and effective. Consider the words of Psalm 149:5-9: "Let the saints be joyful in glory; let them sing aloud on their beds. Let the high praises of God be in their mouth, and a two-edged sword in their hand, to execute vengeance on the nations, and punishments on the peoples; to bind their kings with chains, and their nobles with fetters of iron; to execute on them the written judgment—this honor have all His saints. Praise the LORD!"[14]

Another important reason is explained by Cindy Jacobs,

> When we praise God, He inhabits or enters our praises, and His power overwhelms the power of the enemy. He is a mighty God, and Satan cannot match His strength.

Light will dispel the darkness through God's entering into our praise. Through praise, the Lord Himself begins to do warfare on our behalf to silence our enemy, as we shall see.[15]

Kent Henry, a wonderful prophetic worship leader who bridges the generations, says that "prophetic worship is already in you."[16] Many times he teaches from 1 Samuel 10:5-10. Verses 5 through 7, (*NASB*) reveal:

Afterward you will come to the hill of God where the Philistine garrison is; and it shall be as soon as you come there to the city, that you will meet a group of prophets coming down from the high place with a harp, tambourine, flute, and a lyre before them, and they will be prophesying. Then the Spirit of the LORD will come upon you mightily, and you shall prophesy with them and be changed into another man. It shall be when these signs come to you, do for yourself what the occasion requires, for God is with you.

To "prophesy" comes from the Hebrew word *naba*. This word means to bubble up and speak or sing forth by inspiration. There is usually an ecstasy that moves an individual to prophesy. The Spirit of God grips or seizes you, and an inspiration of God's will comes forth from you. I just say it simply: to prophesy is to speak forth God's mind and heart. Therefore, you have to understand what He's thinking and what He's feeling to express the Lord to those around you.

When people are playing music under divine inspiration and the anointing is flowing, many times prophetic words begin to come forth through an individual in the gathering. These words are powerful. I believe prophetic singing is necessary for some demonic forces to retreat. A good example of this is David and Saul. When David would play, the demons on Saul would let go of him. Kent Henry shares four points on the lifestyle necessary for the spirit of prophecy to flow:

1. The unity factor, both with the Lord and others (2 Chron. 5:13; Acts 2:1);
2. Recognize and be sensitive to the moving of the Holy Spirit (Acts 4:8);
3. Attitudes are vital. Get rid of any legalistic, "Pharisee" spirit. Rejoice always (Phil. 4:6-8); pray without ceasing (Eph. 6:18);
4. Deal with sin quickly in your life (Rom. 2:4).[17]

SING A NEW SONG

In corporate worship, many times individuals will hear a song. Many times the worship leaders want to be spontaneous but know they have a responsibility to keep clear direction and order in the service. What if God gives me a song and there is no avenue for me to give it? This is not uncommon. Many spiritual things are going on during a worship service. Often I draw my pastor and other church leaders up on the platform with me to help administrate the moving of the Holy Spirit in our worship. Those who are in leadership have to assess all those spiritual things and allow the best expression of God's heart to be brought out of it. It is not always easy, and it is not an exact science. We have to trust God to work through the authority structure that He has put in place. If we feel that we have a song but are not able to give it, then we can pray the message of the song. Perhaps God wants that song to be a burden of intercession in you for a season, and when that season is completed, He will make a way for you to release it. You would be surprised how many times I have seen God tell the leader when someone has a song.

John Dickson tells of a story about when he was leading worship one time and the Lord began to stir a song in him. He tells the following:

> But before it had become strong enough for me to release, the worship time had come to an end. Don Crum was the speaker, and when he came to the platform, he said, "The Lord says we are not finished worshiping." The team got back up, and as Don led us back into a powerful time of worship, the song that had been stirring came bubbling back up and I released it in power.

The Lord is well able to make a way for His song. At times we have to be patient and trust in His timing. John also shares a story about his wife, Violet:

> Once the Lord gave my wife, Violet, a song in a service, but there was no opportunity to give it. She didn't get upset or try to push her way in to give it. When we drove home from church that day, I pulled up behind her in our driveway and saw her jump out of her car and dance around our front yard. "Hey John, listen to this song the Lord gave me!" The song had a sassy, Latin sound:

> I will do all that I have spoken
> I will perform by My mighty hand
> I will fulfill what I have purposed
> I will accomplish what I have planned
> For I am God, and there is no other
> For I am God, and there is no one like Me

For I am God, and there is no other
For I am God, and there is no one like Me
I have made known the end from beginning
And I am called the Ancient of Days
I will return in splendor to Zion
And My salvation will not be delayed[18]

Maybe I had missed it at church. In leading worship, sometimes we are not sensitive to what the Lord is saying to others. Maybe I should have discerned that she had this song from the Lord. If so, what can I say? It happens! Lighten up. It's not the end of the world. God is well able to get His message across to us. Later, I wrote the song up with chords and we started singing it in our church services. Eventually we recorded it on one of our CDs, and it has gone out all over the world.

MUSIC IN THE ANOINTING

"The LORD thy God in the midst of thee is mighty; he will save, he will rejoice over thee with joy; he will rest in his love, he will joy over thee with singing" (Zeph. 3:17, *KJV*). How wonderful it is that God rejoices over us with singing!

In his book *The Prophetic Song*, LaMar Boschman writes:

It is of the utmost importance that music be anointed when we sing and play if it is to minister to people and not just be pretty "special" music. Music in the world is performed to impress or to move others emotionally. Christian music can be impressive and stirring, but if the only reason for using it is to impress people and move their emotions we are doing it with the wrong motive.

Something is wrong. God's music goes beyond that. It ministers life and trust because it is presenting and glorifying Jesus. And this can only be done when the musician, the instruments, the singers, and the songs are anointed (that is, saturated in God's Holy Spirit).[19]

The anointing breaks the yoke. I love music with the sound of the Breaker Anointing, which I explain fully later in this book. The higher we go, the clearer the sound. Music helps define the sound of heaven.

And they sang a new song, saying: "You are worthy to take the scroll, and to open its seals; for You were slain,

> As the anointing rises, hear the sound of the Lord and let His song come forth that can break every yoke.

and have redeemed us to God by Your blood out of every tribe and tongue and people and nation, and have made us kings and priests to our God; and we shall reign on the earth." Then I looked, and I heard the voice of many angels around the throne, the living creatures, and the elders; and the number of them was ten thousand times ten thousand, and thousands of thousands, saying with a loud voice: "Worthy is the Lamb who was slain to receive power and riches and wisdom, and strength and honor and glory and blessing!" (Rev. 5:9-12).

As the anointing rises, hear the sound of the Lord and let His song come forth that can break every yoke.

The Keys of Revelation

LeAnn Squier provides a vivid illustration:

The cell group worship we had two weeks ago was a living demonstration of your new book (*The Worship Warrior*). We (about 18 people) came into the Throne Room dimension in a swell of spontaneous worship that lasted well over an hour. I saw that as we worshiped, God summoned angels to come before Him. He placed a scroll in each angel's hand, which I knew contained decrees for answered prayer. Each angel flew (whooshed) away and down in the earthly realm below, decree in hand. I have never seen anything like it.

Much more worship—not just singing, but audible declarations and songs of God's greatness—came up like a ground swell. Some fountain in the deep opened up. When we "finished," we had brief teaching and then prayer. Then again there was a ground swell, this time in prayer, with such great authority that it turned into a roar. It was fearsome. I could no longer stand up. I saw myself running in an open field pursuing the enemy at full tilt. I had a battle axe in one hand and a sword in the other (!). Others were pursuing with me. The enemy was fleeing in every direction. I saw a whole new offensive being launched against the enemy.

In the days following, we started receiving specific, prompt answers to prayers prayed and decrees made that night. Later I realized that we had ascended to the Throne Room and had literally been clothed in authority and boldness that we brought back into the earthly realm. I felt like I had a cloud around my body. It was so strong, that as I talked with a friend afterward she was delivered from a spirit of fear of rejection just from the anointing.

I have experienced this "reclothing" privately, during times of a long fast and intercession, but *never corporately*, and never that quickly. I had never seen or had understanding of just how it happened, until now. Just the phrase "ascending, descending" tells it all.

I believe that a new dimension opened up to the *corporate body* because of the book being written. A door in the heavens has been reopened apostolically.

We must be relentless, impassioned and unwavering in our worship from here on out. The door is open.[20]

THE PARTS ASSEMBLED

No wonder the Word tells us not to forsake the assembling of ourselves together (see Heb. 10:25). We increase in strength, have the power of agreement, the presence of the Lord and the coming together of many gifts to form the corporate Body of Christ. Satan knows this and trembles. He tries everything he can think of to throw a monkey wrench into our corporate gatherings. He works on us as individuals to distract us from joining our faith together as we assemble. So many of us get to church and, instead of pressing in to worship out of our gift and then expressing that worship corporately, we have the following attitudes: "I don't know why, but I'm so depressed today." "Oh no, we're going to sing that song again." "I have so much to do this afternoon." "Boy, am I tired." "I'm soooo sleepy."

John Dickson added:

When I get up to lead worship, I see this. I will even see pockets of 15 or 20 people where a spirit of oppression is concentrated in different areas of the congregation. Sometimes there is a cloud over the whole church. They are hindered, they have the dust of the world on them. The ruler of this world (see John 12:31) has blinded them to who they are and what they can accomplish when they are assembled together.

FOOT WASHING BY JESUS

At the Last Supper, Jesus washed the feet of the disciples (see John 13:3-11). He told them they did not need a bath, that they were already clean. All they needed was to have their feet washed. We are clean, beloved, but too easily our feet get covered with the dust of the world. As we start a corporate worship service, we find it necessary to see this dust by the Spirit and move in a direction that will allow Jesus to wash it off of us.

John Dickson said, "I do not usually start with our most intimate or our most powerful songs. And I do not make mention of the dust; I just begin to point everyone toward Jesus. He said if we would lift Him up, He would draw all men unto Himself (see John 12:32)."

As was coined in the opening of the classic *A Tale of Two Cities*, we are living in the best of times and the worst of times. Worship is the key to these times. Worship leads us into restoration. Receive the sound the Lord is releasing from heaven. Go to war with the sound. Watch the power of loss in your life begin to break from you. Let the Lion of Judah *roar* on your behalf. Roar with Him, and watch restoration begin.

Shake off the dust, shake off the dust
Arise and shine, and be fresh and flourishing

Shake off the dust, shake off the dust
Arise and shine!
For you shall bear fruit in your old age
And you shall see your desire on your enemy
So shake off the dust, shake off the dust
Arise and shine.[21]

Notes

1. Marty Cassady, letter to author, March 19, 2002.
2. Ibid.
3. Billy Graham, *Angels: God's Secret Agents* (New York: Pocket Books, 1975), pp. 32-33.
4. Martin Luther, "A Mighty Fortress Is Our God."
5. *The New Bible Dictionary*, Logos Bible System 2.1 (Bellingham, WA: Logos Research Systems, Inc., 1997).
6. Judith Hann, *How Science Works* (Pleasantville, NY: Dorling Kindersley Limited, 1991), pp. 116, 118.
7. Ernest B. Gentile, *Worship God!* (Portland, OR: City Bible Publishing, 1994), pp. 139-209.
8. *GLIMPSES*, No. 26; *Glimpses* is a bulletin insert published by Christian History Institute, Box 540, Worcester, PA 19490. http://www.gospelcom.net/chi/GLIMPSEF/glimpses/glmps026.shtml.
9. Mark E. Garmeaux, "O Come, Let Us Worship! A Study in Lutheran Liturgy and Hymnology" (presented to the 78th Annual Convention of the Evangelical Lutheran Synod, June 1995), http://www.blc.edu/comm/gargy/gargy1/O_come_let_us_worship.html (accessed August 19, 2002).
10. The Gregorian Association (London, England), *The Gregorian Association (London, England)*, http:www.beaufort.demon.co.uk/chant.htm (accessed August 19, 2002).
11. Terry Law, *The Power of Praise and Worship* (Tulsa, OK: Victory House, Inc., 1985), p. 166.
12. John Dickson, untitled, (Denton, TX: Glory of Zion International Ministries, Inc., 2000).
13. C. Peter Wagner, *Humility* (Ventura, CA: Regal Books, 2002), pp. 7-8.
14. Chuck D. Pierce and Rebecca Wagner Sytsema, *The Best Is Yet Ahead* (Colorado Springs, CO: Wagner Publications, 2001), p. 57.
15. Cindy Jacobs, *Possessing the Gates of the Enemy* (Grand Rapids, MI: Chosen Books, 1991), p. 178.
16. Kent Henry, "Prophetic Worship—Changed into Another Man," 2002.

17. Ibid.

18. Violet Dickson, "For I Am God" (Denton, TX: Glory of Zion International Ministries, Inc., 1998).

19. LaMar Boschman, *The Prophetic Song* (Shippensburg, PA; Destiny Image Publishers, Inc.), p. 31.

20. LeAnn Squier, e-mail message to author, March 25, 2002.

21. LeAnn Squier, "Shake Off The Dust" (Denton, TX: Glory of Zion International Ministries, Inc., 1997).

CHAPTER
8

THE SOUND OF HEAVEN

My word shall go forth as a sword from my mouth
To bind up your infirmities, heal your land
To bind up the strong man proclaim victory
To shatter the darkness, set prisoners free
For I am Jehovah, there is no god beside Me
For I am Jehovah, break forth in victory
I'm pressing the wine press for now is the time
I'm pressing the wine press to bring forth new wine
I'm calling you out for now is the time
I'm calling you out to bring forth new wine
I'm pouring My glory, it's coming down
So drink in My glory, it's all around
I'm pouring My glory, it's coming down
So drink in My glory, it's all around

VIOLET DICKSON, FOR I AM JEHOVAH

In war, there is an order and sound that leads God's people into victory. With the Israelites, the order of battle was simple. The force was drawn up, either in a line, or in three divisions, with a center and two wings. There was a rear guard to provide protection on the march or to bring in stragglers (see Num. 10:25; Josh. 6:9; Judg. 7:16; 1 Sam. 11:11; Isa. 58:8). The signal for the charge and the retreat was given by the sound of a trumpet. There was a battle cry to inspire courage and to impart confidence (see Judg. 7:20; Amos 1:14).

We must have a clear trumpet sound and release of revelation at this time in history. Jesus said that He would build His Church on revelation. Therefore, the Spirit of God must reveal Jesus to us. By the Spirit of God we also have the will of the Lord revealed to us. The Spirit moves over the Word and we understand how to live and walk in today's world.

Only God can reveal Himself to us by His Spirit (Matt. 16). Once we receive revelation, we should begin praying that revelation. Then we move from "praying to saying." Prophetic declaration is very important to change the atmosphere of the heavenlies. We become the trumpet of the Lord in the earth. We are that human shofar.

THE BLAST OF THE TRUMPET

In the Old Testament, the blowing of trumpets heralded the Lord's descent. This sound had great power to jar what seemed invincible.

Once during worship John Dickson began to do an old song in a new way. He sang "Joshua Fight the Battle of Jericho." There is no better biblical example of the sound on Earth of tearing down our powerful foe than Joshua leading the armies of God against Jericho. As John did this song, faith began to rise in the people. Not only did we give an incredible shout that shook the heavens, but the many shofars in the conference came forward and began to blow. Great faith was released.

The trumpet sound preceded the movement of God's presence. This sound warned of approaching danger. This sound was a call to arms. This sound meant redemptive purposes were going to manifest. We find in the book of Revelation, which I will cover later, that as the trumpet sounded there had to be a response. In fact, there are many sounds in the book of Revelation.

Stand, Declare and Make Wisdom Known

The trumpet sound represents a move forward into God's restoration of His purposes on Earth. If the Church will find firm footing, we will see civil government move correctly to overthrow evil. We must take our stand until we see the wall rebuilt that has been broken down in our lives, families, cities, Church and nation.

> **If the Church will find firm footing, we will see civil government move correctly to overthrow evil.**

In Nehemiah, we find worship helped to restore the wall around Jerusalem. The following prayer or prophetic song gives you an idea of how prophetic singing sets a "stand" in the earthly realm:

And the Levites, Jeshua, Kadmiel, Bani, Hashabniah, Sherebiah, Hodijah, Shebaniah, and Pethahiah, said:

"Stand up and bless the LORD your God forever
and ever! Blessed be Your glorious name, which is
exalted above all blessing and praise! You alone are
the LORD; You have made heaven, the heaven of
heavens, with all their host, the earth and everything on it, the seas and all that is in them, and You
preserve them all. The host of heaven worships
You. You are the LORD God, who chose Abram,
and brought him out of Ur of the Chaldeans, and
gave him the name Abraham" (Neh. 9:5-7).

They sang, prophesied and declared the history of Israel
before a covenant-breaking people. They ended by declaring the
following and renewing their covenant:

"Here we are, servants today! And the land that You gave
to our fathers, to eat its fruit and its bounty, here we are,
servants in it! And it yields much increase to the kings
You have set over us, because of our sins; also they have
dominion over our bodies and our cattle at their pleasure; and we are in great distress. And because of all this,
we make a sure covenant, and write it; our leaders, our
Levites, and our priests seal it" (vv. 36-38).

The Plot of the Enemy

We must recognize that we have an enemy who has a plan to
change laws and times so we might be ensnared in his purposes.
Satan's evil plan can be overthrown when we stand and declare
truth. "Do not be afraid or discouraged because of this vast
army. For the battle is not yours, but God's. Tomorrow march
down against them. They will be climbing up by the Pass of Ziz . . .
Take up your positions; stand firm and see the deliverance [of]
the LORD" (2 Chron. 20:15-16, *NIV*).

A Time to Listen

We must have ears to hear the trumpet. We are not used to hearing the way we need to hear right now. God is training our ears to hear.

> The Sovereign LORD has opened my ears, and I have not been rebellious; I have not drawn back (Isa. 50:5, *NIV*).

> Listen to my instruction and be wise; do not ignore it. Blessed is the man who listens to me, watching daily at my doors, waiting at my doorway. For whoever finds me finds life and receives favor from the LORD (Prov. 8:33-35, *NIV*).

> I, John, both your brother and companion in the tribulation and kingdom and patience of Jesus Christ, was on the island that is called Patmos for the word of God and for the testimony of Jesus Christ. I was in the Spirit on the Lord's Day, and I heard behind me a loud voice, as of a trumpet (Rev. 1:9).

Notice that John was on Earth, and his human spirit was so filled with the Holy Spirit that his senses seemed to ascend into heaven. He heard a voice like a trumpet. The voice released vision and revelation that was to be communicated to the Church of that day. The voice not only sounded like a trumpet, but also sounded like many rushing waters. The voice was the voice of the Lord Jesus Christ. The voice commanded him to write what he had seen for the angels of the Church to understand.

We must understand and be able to interpret fully the sound from heaven so that we can communicate by the Spirit what our commander is saying to the Church today. This is truly a time to listen. This sound will be the sound that leads us forth as a mighty kingdom of priests and kings representing the person who releases the sound. Get ready, army. Heaven is sounding, and our Lord and King is preparing to lead us forth.

A Time for War

We must lean in to Him who "changes times and seasons . . . sets up kings and deposes them. He gives wisdom to the wise and knowledge to the discerning. He reveals deep and hidden things; he knows what lies in darkness, and light dwells with him" (Dan. 2:21-22, NIV).

There are three keys to operating in war. First, when it is a time for war, we must go to war. King David had his greatest downfall when during his reign the time came to go to war and he stayed home. Passivity in a time of war is disastrous.

Another key is to know what the war is about. Defining your enemy allows you to gain your victory strategy. We are at war with an enemy who has set himself against the will of God. We will be at war until God's will is done on Earth as it is in heaven. We are at war until we see the Great Commission fulfilled.

In his book *Warfare Prayer*, Dr. C. Peter Wagner puts it this way:

> Satan's primary objective is to prevent God from being glorified by keeping lost people from being saved. Jesus came to seek and to save the lost. God sent His Son that whosoever believes on Him should have everlasting life. Whenever a person is saved, the angels in heaven rejoice. Satan hates all of the above. He wants people to go to hell, not to heaven. And the reason this is his primary objective is that each time he succeeds he has won an *eternal victory*.[1]

In addition to an armed conflict, remember that the definition of war also included an aggressive competition or a struggle to achieve a particular goal. We are seeing tremendously encouraging signs throughout the world. As Dr. Wagner writes in *Praying with Power*, "This is the first time in human history that we have a viable opportunity of completing the Great Commission of Jesus in our generation."[2] The closer we get to winning the war, the more desperate and vicious the kingdom of Satan becomes. It is imperative that we understand our enemy as we move into the future war of the Church.

> The closer we get to winning the war, the more desperate and vicious the kingdom of Satan becomes.

The third key is to war from an abiding place. I never war just to war. I only go to war when I cannot get in my abiding place; or, once in my abiding place, the enemy attempts to remove me from that place of rest, protection and trust that the Almighty has allowed me to experience.

> He who dwells in the secret place of the Most High shall abide under the shadow of the Almighty. I will say of the LORD, "He is my refuge and my fortress; My God, in Him I will trust" (Ps. 91:1-2).

Wow! That clearly describes worship and war. Once we are in our abiding place, all of the incredible promises listed in Psalm 91 are available to us.

Ascend, Worship, Hear and Then Walk

As I noted earlier, worship takes us through steps of ascension into the heavenly realms. The Lord Jesus Christ then mediates our arrival into the Throne Room, where we have the incredible privilege of standing boldly before a holy God. As we ascend, we gain more and more revelation of who He is and what His will is for our lives on Earth.

We are positioned in the heavens, but we walk on Earth (see Eph. 1–2). When we know our abiding place in the heavenlies, we walk with great confidence and faith. We go to war when the enemy tries to pull us out of that abiding place or block us from ascending to that abiding place in Christ. We often feel this blockade as we ascend in worship. This is when it's necessary to express the sound of war from our spirits toward the enemy. Remember, we are worshiping all the way into the Throne Room.

After having full revelation of the state of the Church of that historical time, the following happened to John. A door opened! Revelation 4:1 records the event: "After these things I looked, and behold, a door standing open in heaven. And the first voice which I heard was like a trumpet speaking with me, saying, 'Come up here, and I will show you things which must take place after this.' "

This released much more revelation to John. The Lord asked John to come in. So not only did he come up, but he came in. The Lord then began to give him the heavenly perspective of things that would take place on Earth.

Revelation 5:9 continues: "And they sang a new song, saying: 'You are worthy to take the scroll, and to open its seals; for You were slain, and have redeemed us to God by Your blood out of every tribe and tongue and people and nation." There is a realm of worship where revelation becomes unsealed. Once this revelation begins to enter into our spirit, the strategy of the revelation causes us to walk in full victory on Earth.

Revelation shows us a pattern of what gets released to us in the Throne Room when we worship:

1. God breaks open the seals! He releases future judgments on the earth. As we worship, He releases vengeance on the enemies that have been resisting you as His beloved child. He also releases judgments on those who are resisting His covenant purposes. We don't have the right to judge, but we have the right to worship. From our worship, He releases judgments.

2. There is a release of trumpets and a prophetic anointing. Revelation 19:10 declares, "And I fell at his feet to worship him. But he said to me, 'See that you do not do that! I am your fellow servant, and of your brethren who have the testimony of Jesus. Worship God! For the testimony of Jesus is the spirit of prophecy.'"

3. Jesus releases "woes" on Earth. Matthew 23 and 24 list these woes. His first woe came to the scribes and Pharisees. When we worship, we break the power of religious spirits over our lives. We can then receive the prophetic revelation and truth God sends today. Proverbs 29:18 in *The Amplified Bible* reads, "Where there is no vision [no redemptive revelation of God], the people perish; but he who keeps the law [of God, which includes that of man]—blessed (happy, fortunate, and enviable) is he." Many people do not understand prophecy because they do not understand God's redemptive purpose. When we worship, He releases His Word and redemptive purpose for our lives today. If we will worship, we will not reject prophetic revelation and wisdom as the scribes and Pharisees did.

Jesus then released a woe over Jerusalem. If we will worship over our cities, we will see our time of visitation. He said in Matthew 24:6-8, "And you will hear of wars and rumors of wars. See that you are not troubled; for all these things must come to pass, but the end is not yet. For nation will rise against nation, and kingdom against kingdom. And there will be famines, pestilences and earthquakes in various places. All these things are the beginning of sorrows." However, he added, "But he who endures to the end shall be saved" (v. 13). To "endure" is to hold one's ground in conflict and to hold up against adversity. To endure is to stand under stress and, as found in Ephesians 6, to stand firm. To endure is to persevere under pressure while we wait calmly and courageously for the Lord to intervene. This is an energetic resistance toward our enemy as we draw near to the Lord and intimately worship Him.

4. He releases the bowls full of prayer and full of wrath! Intercession and worship are so important. The saints' praying causes bowls in heavens to fill. Revelation 5:8 reads, "Now when He had taken the scroll, the four living creatures and the twenty-four elders fell down before the Lamb, each having a harp, and gold bowls full of incense, which are the prayers of the saints." When our prayers ascend, they are purified. The smell and fragrance of redemption laces true spirit-filled praying. While our prayers are ascending, angelic forces descend to set guard over our mouth and watch over the door of our lips (see Ps. 141:3-4). What is in our heart proceeds out of our mouth. As our prayers ascend and fill the bowl, He fills our hearts. Revelation 16 has a list of the bowls. Once the bowls are full from

the saints' prayers, God begins to set Earth in order. He judges the beast and those who worship his image. As the bowls are filled, we see a pattern from heaven that is similar to what Moses and the Israelites experienced before pharaoh. Modern day pharaohs are judged through the saints' worship. When we ascend in worship, we have the right to tell Babylon to break and fall. The powers of sorcery, lying and abominable perverse spirits break on Earth as we worship.

5. New songs from heaven are released to Earth. I'll cover this later.

6. When we ascend in worship, we have supernatural protection in spiritual warfare. All of the blessings of Psalm 91 are available to us because we enter into our abiding place. When we ascend, we can stand against the demonic forces that Christ has already defeated through His ascension. They are under His feet. And as we ascend in worship, we move from our earthly condition into our heavenly position. True victory in warfare occurs when we get our feet planted on our enemies. Warfare is not yelling at the devil. It's placing our feet on top of his purposes that are set against our victory and Jesus' influence in the earth.

7. Worship releases an awareness of the Lamb on the Throne:
   a. His intimate relationship with us;
   b. His ministry to the earthly realm;
   c. His divine government;
   d. His missions call.

Authority in Worship and Revelation

The Lord told Peter that the gates of hell would not prevail against him. He also told him that He would build His Church upon the divine revelation that Peter had just experienced from the Father. We build the Church through prophetic revelation and then the gates of hell have no right to prevail. If you build with God's pattern in the earth, you will overcome hell. If you build properly by revelation you will receive keys to the Kingdom. Remember, we do not build the Kingdom. It's the kingdom of the Lord. This is what causes many people problems; they actually attempt to take the Father's revelation and build their own Kingdom. You receive keys to unlock the Kingdom. If we build the Church properly, you will get keys so you can unlock the Kingdom. The Kingdom has to do with the rule, reign and authority of God. Apostolic gifting, authority and proper alignment of the saints in a territory constitute Kingdom blessings being released. This is not the local church. The Kingdom represents each gift and each "tribe" of believers aligning together in their territory to represent the rule of God. This is what presents wisdom to powers and principalities in your territory. Binding and loosing are related to the Kingdom. If you build right, you have the Kingdom authority to forbid and permit. The only way you can gain this type of authority is to worship.

Elijah was a man like us. He had the same type of emotional makeup as we do. We find James 5 telling us this. We can learn much from his example of exercising authority. Remember, he gave a word to the civil authorities of his day. That word set a course in heaven that affected the earth (see 1 Kings 17). However, we also find him watching after that word so that when it was God's time to perform in the earth, he went into intercession until the will of God in heaven began to manifest in the earth. What gave him, and what will give us, the right to exercise the authority of God in the earthly realm? Let's look at this pattern found in 1 Kings 18.

1. He knew God's timing of revelation.
2. He understood the promise of God.

3. He understood that the timing of God was linked with the manifestation of the promise.

4. He understood the power of prophetic declaration. He knew he could call forth the will of God from heaven and that God's will would eventually manifest in the earth. The Lord had said it would not rain for three years. That time frame was up. It was time for rain. He had to come into agreement with this revelation and begin to pray.

5. He understood his position before God. That was a position of humility. This is where worship enters in.

6. He had great perseverance before God. He did not give up.

7. He stayed in intercession until what he knew was in the heavens manifested on the earth.

8. He expected God to answer. Therefore, the expectations in his emotions stayed in right alignment with God's purposes. He resisted the hope deferred and disappointments of Israel's shortcomings, and prayed and worshiped until change occurred.

Psalms of Ascent

Many times we forget that through worship, restoration and victory occur. I have many people all over the world with whom I align who love to worship, pray and intercede. In my home church, we set aside every Wednesday to pray all day. We pray and worship throughout the day and then meet corporately at night. During the day we also have a room set aside for healing, deliverance and restoration. We know that we can ascend, worship, impart God's anointing and see people's lives restored.

David taught us this through the Psalms of ascent. Linda Heidler, one of the pastors of our church, did a study one morning on the Psalms of ascent as she prepared for the all-day Wednesday service.

1. **Psalm 120** begins the ascent with the people in trouble and crying out to God. They are surrounded by lying and deceit and are being shot at with flaming arrows. The solution is to ascend to the Lord in Zion.

2. **Psalm 121** is the actual beginning of the ascent at the foot of Mount Zion. As they look at the mountain, they say, "I will need help for this climb. Where will it come from?" Like the children of Israel when leaving Egypt, they say if the Lord does not help us, we cannot do this. The Lord will not allow my foot to slip. He will keep me, protect me and guard me as I go out and as I come in.

3. In **Psalm 122** they focus on the joy set before them of entering the gates of Jerusalem. This is a Psalm of praise and joy and worship. Through these Psalms there is a cycle of crying for help, being delivered and ascending higher until they fully arrive.

4. In **Psalm 123** as they ascend they cry out for God's helping hand. This is a prayer—they are under attack again by those who are not climbing, but are at ease. They begin to scoff at them with contempt. Those who are ascending look to the Lord.

5. In **Psalm 124** the battle becomes fiercer. Men rise up against them, set traps and snares for them, rage at them and try to overwhelm them. Had it not been for the Lord on their side, they would have been swallowed alive.

6. In **Psalm 125** the psalmist finally climbs to and escapes the traps and snares. They are as strong as Mount Zion and will not be moved. They escape the

scepter of wickedness. The plan of evil authority cannot rest on them. The land begins to rejoice in this place of ascension.

7. In **Psalm 126** they again turn their attention to the joy of entering Zion. The power of remembrance of joy comes upon them. This is a place of "coming home." Deliverance begins to abound. A divine release comes at this place. The presence of God and rejoicing is so strong that it's hard for them even to believe that they have broken out of their grief.

8. In **Psalms 127 and 128** a new distraction arises— worry and concern about their cities, homes and children they have had to leave in order to ascend. The Lord answers by assuring them that unless he watches their city, they watch in vain, and unless he builds their house, they labor in vain. Their children will be like arrows in the hand of a warrior and will not go off course, but will hit the mark. Their homes will be filled with blessing and prosperity.

9. **Psalm 129** brings a new and even more vicious attack. However, because they have ascended, they have new strength that they received back in Psalm 125. Therefore, the attack is short-lived and their enemies are put to shame. They begin to clothe themselves with blessings and favor.

10. In **Psalm 130**, they stand in the presence of God receiving grace and forgiveness. Their past is removed. Hope arises new and fresh. The assurance of redemption rests upon them, and the power of iniquity begins to break. They know they must touch God, so they will let go of anything to touch Him.

11. In **Psalms 131–134** the people come to the place of perfect peace. They have stopped striving and leaning

on their own understanding concerning their circumstances, have allowed trust to arise and have embraced the faithful love of God. As a weaned child rests against his mother's breast, my soul is a weaned child within me. A weaned child has come to a new place of maturity. There is no peace until all our enemies are under our feet. They have ascended above their enemies as they have reached the goal of the Throne Room. They sing, praise and worship in the presence of the Lord. Arise, O Lord, to thy resting place. Unity and the anointing begin to flow. "How good and pleasant it is for brothers to dwell together (worship) in unity" (133:1, *NASB*). There is a new anointing, like the oil poured on Aaron's head and flowing down to the hem of his robe. There is a new refreshing like the dew of Hermon on the Mountains of Zion. In that place the Lord commands the blessing of life! Every place of death is overcome by the command of the Lord bringing life. The command of the Lord cannot be resisted or opposed. His Word accomplishes what He sends it out to do. The end result is glorious praise to God all night long.

DISTRACTIONS: THE ENEMIES OF WORSHIP

John Dickson said:

Sometimes I have thought of ascending in worship like floating on a cloud up to the Throne Room. I had not seen the battle of ascending. The key is to have a heart to keep ascending and not turn back or get sidetracked. It is the attitude that I will take care of what is in my way so that I can continue my climb. The focus is never off of the goal. The goal is the Throne Room, the presence of God and to be engulfed by His glory.

Distraction keeps us from really worshiping and accomplishing what God would have us build. Each one of us has a plan of building for our life. We are also part of building and restoring what God wants us to restore in the earth. He connects us with some covenant vision. However, to build properly we cannot get distracted.

> The goal is the Throne Room, the presence of God and to be engulfed by His glory.

Jesus taught us the importance of worship versus distractions. I love the story of Jesus visiting the home of Mary and Martha. Martha welcomed Him into her house. Once He was there, Mary sat at His feet and listened to His word. Martha was proud of her home and glad to have the Lord visiting. However, she missed the purpose of His visit. He was not there on a social visit, but to release His word to the city of Bethany. Luke 10:40 says, "Martha was distracted with much serving." The word "distracted" in Greek is *perispao*, which means to be encumbered and dragged all around.

Mary, on the other hand, seemed to stay very focused on the highest purpose of the moment. Martha even approached the Lord and said, "Lord, do You not care that my sister has left me to serve alone?" (Luke 10:40). In other words, "Make my sister come drag around in circles with me!" As a matter of fact, she even told the Lord what to do. Jesus answered and said to her, "Martha, Martha, you are worried and troubled about many things. But one thing is needed, and Mary has chosen that good part which will not be taken away from her" (Luke 10:41).

In *The Best Is Yet Ahead* by Rebecca Sytsema and myself, we write:

> This is a time in history when all of the events around us could get us distracted from the highest purpose of God. We have enough with our daily lives and all the cares of the world placed upon us. In the Greek the word "worry" is *merimnao*. This word means "to divide in parts." The word also suggests a distraction, a preoccupation with things causing anxiety, stress, pressure, and the straying from the focused goal that we are called to accomplish.[3]

Distraction and worry can fragment us. Martha got preoccupied, whereas Mary got focused. What brought Mary into focus was her worship. Martha's distraction put her in danger of missing the best that God had for her. It was not that Martha never worshiped. The fact was that she just got distracted and preoccupied instead of taking the opportunity to gain necessary revelation for her future. We must work when God says work, but we need to be intimate when we have the opportunity to be intimate. Whatever we are doing, we need to stay focused.

I love the book *Distractions from Destiny*, by Harry and Cheryl Salem. They lay out eight key distractions that deviate us from the presence of God and the goals that He has for us.

1. Broken focus; thoughts and emotions are powerful forces that can easily break our focus and distract us from our destiny.

2. People; relationships with dream stealers or those who don't share the same dream can destroy your destiny.
3. An offended heart; an offended heart will drag you down and cause you to stumble on your way to destiny.
4. Double-mindedness.
5. Lack of direction; if we do not have a good road map or clear directions, we may find ourselves wandering on every back road along the way.
6. Time; we must be patient as we wait for our destiny to be fulfilled.
7. The comparison trap; jealousy and discontent sidetrack many from reaching their full potential.
8. Fear.[4]

I call these "worship robbers." They rob us of worshiping God. Look at Philippians 3:14: "I press toward the mark for the prize of the high calling of God in Christ Jesus" (*KJV*). The apostle Paul tells us to press toward the mark. The word "press" implies action, discipline and an ongoing pursuit. But that's where some people fall short since they are not willing to continue in their pursuit. Jerry Savelle shares:

When you lose focus, you become disillusioned. It causes you to lose sight over your vision. Hebrews 12:1 says, "Lay aside every weight, and the sin which doth so easily beset us . . . " To win, you have to get rid of the "weights" that are pulling you down. You have to look to Jesus and away from everything else. Focused people are not easily distracted. Focused people refuse to compromise what they believe. They make no provision for failure. Focused people do not easily change what they believe because of the circumstances. Focused people finish what they start. They will not give up. What is the "mark" you're pressing toward? Whatever it is, each day that you press toward it, you're getting a little closer.[5]

Savelle goes on to share four ways to stay focused:

1. Stay in the Word. God's Word builds you up. When do you need to be strong the most? In a trial. The Word to a believer is like spinach to Popeye. When you stay in the Word, your faith gets built up.
2. Stay in faith. Faith is what enables you to overcome the world. Check yourself and see what has been coming out of your mouth lately. When you are in faith, you do not talk negative.
3. Stay in fellowship. Fellowship with the Holy Ghost puts you in a position of advantage. It keeps you in contact with headquarters.
4. Stay in joy. Do not get so bogged down with believing that you lose your joy. Be determined to keep your joy no matter what happens. In the presence of the Lord there is fullness of joy."[6]

The only way you can do this is to stay in worship. Keep ascending! In the psalms, David brings the reality of how the dust of the world can overtake us and cause us to lose our luster in God. "My heart is in anguish within me" (Ps. 55:4, *NASB*). "I have sunk into deep mire, and there is no foothold" (Ps. 69:2, *NASB*). "My heart has been smitten like grass and has withered away" (Ps. 102:4, *NASB*). But as his psalms would unfold, he would begin to move out of that dusty place and express confidence in God and His ability to deliver. Then he would usually launch into great proclamations with praise and worship. David had these psalms sung in the Tabernacle. He knew that if individuals would begin to worship and praise God in the sanctuary, the dust would actually be blown from them by God's wonderful Spirit.

Be Strengthened for War

Let the Lord dust off your weapons. "Beat your plowshares into swords and your pruning hooks into spears. Let the weakling say, 'I am strong!' " (Joel 3:10, *NIV*). Our weapons of war are to be made into instruments of peace. However, this verse actually says to take the implements they were using for agriculture and make them into weapons of war. Therefore, we see symbolic language. Verse 11 reads, "Assemble and come, all you nations, and gather together all around. Cause your mighty ones to go down there, O LORD." In other words, if we'll come together and let our weapons of war be fashioned for the future, He will send His angelic forces or heavenly armies to assist us as we go forth into the warfare ahead. "Let the nations be wakened, and come up to the Valley of Jehoshaphat; for there I will sit to judge all the surrounding nations. Put in the sickle, for the harvest is ripe. Come, go down; for the winepress is full, the vats overflow—for their wickedness is great" (vv. 12-13).

Come up, and then go down. Let the Lord cleanse you from everything that would keep you from ascending and then going forth to war with a clear conscience. What will He cleanse as you ascend?

1. Presumption—faith is the center pole. Doubt and unbelief are on one extreme and presumption is on the other. Presumption is speaking beyond your level of faith, beyond the bounds of your faith
2. Insecurity
3. Inferiority—you have not recognized who you are in Christ
4. Rejection
5. Pride

We have a prophetic filter, the conscience, like a window between the soul and the spirit. If the soul is not submitted to the Spirit, then what is in it will filter through into the prophetic. This window is being cleansed the higher we go. Finally, in God's presence it's like we have been in a vacuum that has removed all impurity.

Be strengthened as you ascend. Most people think that as they go up they lose strength. Actually, it's just the opposite. We sing several songs that contain this phrase: "Let the weak say, 'I am strong.'" The location of this verse is very interesting. In the context of Scripture, it refers to people who are getting themselves ready to go to war. It is an exhortation for those who feel

Ascending in Worship

The Spirit of God is prophetically telling the Body of Christ to declare, "We are warriors."

Descending in War

too weak to go out and fight. We need to arouse ourselves by declaring that they are strong. This was a Scripture passage given for warriors. As a matter of fact, the word translated "strong" is the Hebrew word *gibbor*. It means warrior or tyrant. The verse actually says, Let the weak say, "I am a warrior." The Spirit of God is prophetically telling the Body of Christ to declare, "We are warriors."

Satan Gets Nervous

He is the prince of the world. Therefore, he has been at work to suppress, oppress and depress the congregation before we assemble together. So when we come together, we should not be surprised if the congregation is less than on fire. By the time we gather together for our corporate gathering, the enemy has been at work all week to isolate and disconnect us from each other and from the Lord. He fears the corporate gathering. John shared that when he begins to lead worship, he knows that "by faith I turn their eyes toward Jesus with music. It's not necessarily the tempo of the song or its lyrics. It is the reliance on God's gift and His anointing to accomplish His purposes. This washes the feet of the individuals and brings them together as a Body."

As the Body begins to unite, Satan begins to get nervous. He knows that as they join their faith, they will have increased strength against him. They will have the power of agreement in their prayers. The presence of the Lord will be in their midst, and the different gifts among them will join together to form the Body of Christ, which has the power of the "head" to overcome His purposes on Earth.

Look at the distractions that Satan brings during corporate worship. John says he seems to see these thoughts going on in people's minds as he leads worship: "Quick, look over there at that dress Mrs. Smith is wearing. Isn't that gaudy?" "Oh, there goes Mr. Smith. He hurt my feelings last month and has never apologized." "I hope church doesn't go long today; the game starts at noon." However, as we ascend together and the Body begins to join in love with each other, the Lord begins to wash our feet. The captain of the host comes into our midst. God ordained us to assemble, and not to forsake the assembling, since He knows this will undo the enemy's plan.

Paul called Satan the god of this world (see 2 Cor. 4:4, NASB). The Earth is the Lord's (see Ps. 24:1), but the world system is ruled by Satan. That is why Jesus said the world would hate believers and the Church (see John 15:18). It hated Him first, of course. We can expect those powers to hate us and resist us, but we are given power to tread upon them (see Luke 10:19).

Worship is a weapon we have in order to do that. When David worshiped with his harp in the presence of King Saul, the evil spirit that was oppressing Saul could not abide in the presence of the anointing that was in David's worship (see 1 Sam. 16:14-23). We need to allow that anointing to be loosed in our praise that will push back the forces of the prince of this world. But here is where we often stop as worshipers. We get the dust washed off of our feet and the ground-level demons pushed back. We are able to release the love we have in our hearts toward God and receive His love, His assurance and affirmation—to praise Him and worship Him, bask in His presence, enjoy His Spirit. But this is a day God wants us to do more. He wants us to ascend in worship, to war in the heavenlies, to make known to the rulers and powers His manifold wisdom. Paul tells us that it is the Church that Jesus uses to preach God's wisdom to demonic powers in the midheavens "so that the manifold wisdom of God might now be made known *through the church* to the rulers and the authorities in the heavenly places" (Eph. 3:10, *NASB*, emphasis added).

Robert Gay, in his book *Silencing the Enemy*, writes:

> Music and worship have played an integral role in the church throughout history. A study of church music and worship reveals that God has restored different elements of worship progressively. He has led the church from glory to glory through fresh revelation from heaven. As the church was changed and conformed to what God was saying in times past, so we must change and conform to what He is saying today. . . . An in-depth study of Church history also illustrates that with every move of God came changes in the way worship was expressed. . . . Without a

revelation of what God is saying concerning worship in this hour, we will be like the children of Israel who wandered in the wilderness for forty years and died. But as we joyfully receive and enter into the revelation of the Spirit, we will be like those who crossed the Jordan and obtained their promised possession.[7]

So many times we are only concerned about ourselves. This is a time that God is bringing us into a kingdom perspective. A kingdom has a King. We need to exalt our King over Earth. The Lord is with us! In the Bible, war always had a religious significance. Since Israel was the firstfruits of God and His inheritance, the priests reminded their armies that Yahweh was with them to fight their battles (see Deut. 20:1-4). To open a campaign, or to enter an engagement, the priest performed sacrificial rites (see 1 Sam 7:8-10; 13:9). If the people *prepared for war* and made the appropriate sacrifices to a holy God, this would sanctify the war they were entering (see Jer. 6:4; 22:7; 51:27,28; Joel 3:9-10). Isaiah 13:3 declares that Yahweh gathers His host and summons to battle His "consecrated [set apart] ones" (*NASB*). The warriors, consecrated by the sacrifices offered before the war, actually were the forerunners in battle. The Lord is calling out His forerunners. There is a holy sanctification going on in the Body as He prepares us to stand against the forces that are holding captive our families, churches and cities.

Worship and Intercession
In *My Utmost for His Highest*, Oswald Chambers writes:

Worship and intercession must go together, the one is impossible without the other. Intercession means that we rouse ourselves up to get the mind of Christ about the one for whom we pray. Too often instead of worshiping God, we construct statements as to how prayer works. Are we worshiping or are we in dispute with God—"I don't see how You are going to do it." This is a sure sign that we are not worshiping. When we lose sight of God we become hard and dogmatic. We hurl our own petitions at God's throne and dictate to Him as to what we wish Him to do. We do not worship God, nor do we seek to form the mind of Christ. If we are hard towards God, we will become hard toward other people. Are we worshiping God that we rouse ourselves up to lay hold on Him so that we may be brought into contact with His mind about the ones for whom we pray? Are we living in a holy relationship to God, or are we hard and dogmatic? "But there is no one interceding properly"— then be that one yourself, be the one who worships God and who lives in holy relationship to Him. Get into the real work of intercession, and remember it is a work, a work that taxes every power; but a work which has no snare. Preaching [the] gospel has a snare; intercessory prayer has none.[8]

When we worship and intercede, we tear down the snares that have been erected in the earth by our enemy. God has a process of manifesting His will on Earth. Worship invades each one of the steps of that process. The process is as follows:

1. **Intercessory burden**. God releases His burden from heaven. One of the words related to intercession is "burden bearing." This means to sustain, bear or hold up against a thing. Dutch Sheets writes that "this is likened to when a person will tie a stake to a tomato plant to sustain it from the weight it carries. The strength of the stake is transferred to

the plant, and thus, 'bears' it up."[9] Sheets goes on to write that another word for burden is " 'to bear, lift or carry' something with the idea being to carry it *away* or *remove* it. . . . The intercessory work of Christ reached its fullest and most profound expression when our sins were 'laid on' Him and He bore 'them' away."[10] Therefore, the Lord will lay His burden on us for something in the earthly realm, and we are to stand and pray until we get rid of it. I do not believe we can withstand this burden without intimate worship.

2. **Revelation Released**. When we are bearing the burden of the Lord, we are *lifting* that burden up to Him for change. He begins to release revelation to us that will give us strategy to see the individual or the city or

---

When we are bearing the burden of the Lord, we are lifting that burden up to Him for change.

---

the nation or the situation change. The Holy Spirit begins to help us. He is our advocate. He is our comforter. He is our helper. He is our counselor. He is our intercessor. He helps us in our weakness, so we can withstand the weight of this burden. When we don't know how to pray, He reveals the will of the Father to us. This is another way of saying what we find in Romans 8:26-28: Revelation can come to us naturally or supernaturally. But it only comes when we touch God in some way or form of intimate worship—whether it be reading the Bible, walking and praying, singing or whatever.

3. **Prophetic Declaration.** Once we have revelation, we can make declaration. We can call things as they should be. The Lord formed the world by faith. As we ascend in worship, faith abounds. We can then speak what is not into the form that it should be. This is the creative power of the Word when filled with Christ's life. As we worship we hear, and the life of God abounds in the earth.

4. **Apostolic Execution.** Once the Word and will of God are being released in heaven, our burden begins to lift. The gifts of the apostles are key in days ahead. Apostolic authority is key to establishing God's will in the earth. Apostles have territorial authority. They also execute the prophetic will of the Lord in the earthly realm. Apostles are called to worship and war.

5. **Divine Fulfillment.** One of the gifts of the apostle is the gift of building. Once God has released His will from heaven, we have interceded and stood in the gap to see that will established, we've made prophetic declarations, and apostolic leadership has gone forth into new vision, then we begin to see the divine will of God fulfilled in the earth. We then drop on our knees and worship and thank God.

The Law of Lift and the Breaker Anointing

John Dickson says:

We have intercessors who meet before each service and during the week. They seek the Lord for discernment of the schemes of the enemy and the strategies needed to overcome them. They stand in the gap and pray. They pray for the leaders to hear God in the service. They pray for the people to be able to break through. This helps me, as a worship leader, to be able to hear the Lord as I lead the people in the service. Sometimes, as I move through my list of songs, it is exactly what I need to ascend and break through. But sometimes it is not, and the Lord directs me to depart from my list and go another direction. The pastor and the other leaders are a part of this as well. They come to the stage as they hear direction from the Lord. Together, we listen to the captain of the hosts as He directs us in battle to break through the barriers of the enemy."

There are two natural laws that oppose each other in the world: the law of gravity and the law of lift. When an aircraft sits stationary, the law of gravity holds it securely to the ground, but as it begins to roll down a runway, the aerodynamics of the wing design causes another natural law to come into play, the law of lift. As the aircraft increases speed on the runway, the two natural laws war until, if the wings are designed right, the law of lift overcomes the law of gravity. As the church ascends in worship, the strategies and direction of the Lord in our service are like the law of lift, enabling us to break the hold of gravity on us and open the corridor through the heavenly places.

So as we praise, proclaim, worship, war and celebrate, the forces of hell on Earth are dispelled and we begin to ascend in worship. Let's review what begins to happen as we ascend. We begin to war the powers of darkness, taking authority and making known to them the wisdom of God, forcing them to clear that corridor between heaven and Earth.

Angels are sent to war on our behalf like they were for Daniel. The writer of Hebrews tells us that angels are "ministering spirits, sent out to render service for us" (Heb. 1:14, *NASB*).

The Breaker Anointing goes before us; Jesus leads us in triumphal entry. As we praise, God Himself comes down that corridor to inhabit and enthrone Himself on our praises (see Ps. 22:3). Woe to the principality that tries to stand his ground in that corridor when God is coming through. As we break through the heavens, God begins to release things to His Church. They begin to flow down: gifts, revelations, strategies, prophetic mantles, tongues and interpretations, healing, deliverance and more.

It is not that it is impossible to experience any of these things without a worship service, but it is my experience that all of these things and more have a much freer and more powerful avenue to flow when we join together and worship our worthy God. When we as individual Christians join to become the corporate Body of Christ; when the power of agreement comes into play; when the different giftings combine; when God squeezes the "cluster" of grapes to make one wine (see Isa. 65:8, *NASB*); when the heavens are open, there is an increased anointing that looses the power of God to His people.

This kind of service should be our daily fare as God's Church. He is not lacking in what He longs to pour out on His Church, nor is He stingy. But He desires that we operate in faith and in the gifts and anointings He has appropriated for us. Our own talents and musical abilities will not ruffle the kingdom of darkness nor thwart its oppression of God's people. Darlene Zschech writes in her book *Extravagant Worship*:

> Praise and worship breaks all boundaries of talent and ability because IT INVADES HELL AND EXCITES HEAVEN! We must think way beyond notes, form or technique. Praise and worship is a powerful expression

of love that transcends the possibilities of music. It is given to us as a weapon of warfare . . . or as a warm blanket on a cold night.[11]

Our skills and talents can only take us so far in such a calling. We must be willing for God to endue us with power (see Luke 24:49) to train our hands for war (see Ps. 144:1). Leading God's people in opening the heavens is no insignificant undertaking. We are not pitted against pushovers in the heavenly places, and to be victorious against them we must know who we are in Christ and who it is that has commissioned us. Darlene goes on in her book to write: "Undergird everything that the pastor is doing and help him to bring in the net."[12]

John Dickson says:

God's worship leaders are not called to sing a few rousing songs to warm up the crowd. We are commissioned to colabor with the man or woman of God to open the heavens and make a way for the Presence of God to come and the Word of God to be released to His people that they might be freed from encumbrances, drawn into the Kingdom and equipped for the work God has called them to. It is a joy to me and a safeguard to colabor with my pastor and other leaders in a worship service. It is not all given to me to break us through. Sometimes, God will stop me from doing anything in a service. His Spirit holds me back from singing or speaking. I begin to look around because I know He has told someone else to do something. Sure enough, as I back off, God moves someone else up to bring forth something.

Once He just told me to duck. It was one of those moments in the presence of God. We were in silence. The air was pregnant. God was wanting to bring something

forth to the congregation. The person He was speaking
to was not wanting to step into the place God was
requiring him to stand in, and as long as I was standing on the stage, he felt God would use me or someone
else to do the job. When God told me to duck, I knew
what God was wanting. I knew who had the word and
that he was not wanting to come up. I simply laid down
on the stage and the person could see the word was not
going to be given unless he got up and did it. It was a
powerful word, and it broke things through for the
congregation. We are a body and God wants each of us
to function as our particular part so that the whole
body might be complete. How good it is and how
pleasant for brothers to dwell together in unity. It is
like the oil poured over the beard, even Aaron's beard,
when the oil poured down (see Ps. 133). There is a special anointing when we operate in unity as one body. It
pleases the Father.

Baal-Perazim: A Place of Breakthrough

The enemy attempts to set barriers so we cannot break through
into the fullness God has for us. We can see a principal here that
when that barrier in the midheavens is breached, things are able
to be released on Earth: revelation, prophetic words, gifts and all
the things God desires to pour upon His church. Paul writes,
"But thanks be to God, who always leads us in triumph in
Christ, and manifests through us the sweet aroma of the knowledge of Him in every place" (2 Cor. 2:14, *NASB*).

God wants to lead us in breaking through this barrier our
enemy has set against us. This word "triumph" is from the Greek
word *thriambeuo* (three-am-byoo'-o), which denotes a grand triumphal entry. God wants to lead us in a grand triumphal procession through that corridor of demonic resistance.

I will surely assemble all of you, Jacob, I will surely gather the remnant of Israel. I will put them together like sheep in the fold; like a flock in the midst of its pasture. They will be noisy with men. The breaker goes up before them; they break out, pass through the gate and go out by it. So their king goes on before them, and the LORD at their head (Mic. 2:12-13, *NASB*).

Micah describes the Lord as "the Breaker," who will break us through the gates of resistance. The word "breaker" here is the Hebrew word *parats* (paw-rats) which is interestingly used in the book of Samuel. Barbara Yoder explains this in her book *The Breaker Anointing*:

In 1 Samuel 3:1 there is an example of breaking though. This passage is about the transition from an old system to a new one. Because of compromise on Eli's part, revelation was shut up. The second part of verse 1 says: "And the word of the LORD was precious in those days; there was no open vision" (*KJV*). The New King James says, "there was no widespread revelation." The Hebrew word for open or widespread is *parats*, the same word for break out. The implication is that something has to be broken through for revelation to be released. But here in 1 Samuel, there was no breakthrough revelation. There was no revelation that was breaking them out of where they were. They were stuck.[13]

God wants to lead us in breaking through where there is no revelation, no prophecy, no gifts flowing, when we are stuck. Yoder gives an account of a worship service that experienced this breakthrough:

While the musicians were playing after I spoke, I had a vision. In the vision I saw a glass ceiling. The people beneath the ceiling could see through the glass to where they need to go, [but] they were unable to penetrate the ceiling. They had vision because they could see where they were supposed to head. However the glass represented a wall that had been raised up against them to keep them from moving into God's place for them. Suddenly the glass began to shatter and I could see and hear the pieces of glass "chink" as they hit the floor. The glass ceiling was shattering. That was a spiritual vision, a picture of what God was doing right then. As the vision came to an end, one of the singers began breaking forth into a new song that had never been sung before. As the song rang out, a great spirit of revelation began to break out on those that were at the meeting. That which had been obstructing their forward progress was removed.[14]

David understood this breakthrough from a military perspective. When an enemy has you hemmed in, held back and confined, you must press against that force in such a manner

---

To break through the evil powers
that hinder us in the heavens, we
must seek the Lord for strategy.

---

that will break its hold. David knew God as the Breaker, Baal-Perazim (the Lord of breakthrough) in 1 Chronicles. "David said, 'God has broken through my enemies by my hand, like the breakthrough of waters.' Therefore they named that place Baal-Perazim" (1 Chron. 14:11, *NASB*). David also understood break-through in the heavens. He assailed the heavens with praise and proclamations and taught his worship leaders to do the same. To break through the evil powers that hinder us in the heavens, we must seek the Lord for strategy. May the Breaker Anointing lead you forth into the place of victory that God has for you!

Restoration of the Tabernacle of God

As we have crossed into the new millennium, so much is being said and taught about the restoration of the Tabernacle of David. It is a promise and a prophecy.

> On that day I will raise up the tabernacle of David, which has fallen down, and repair its damages; I will raise up its ruins, and rebuild it as in the days of old; that they may possess the remnant of Edom, and all the Gentiles who are called by My name (Amos 9:11-12).

This verse was quoted in Acts 15 to set a course for the Church today. It's necessary to see restoration of the areas that David installed in worship to see the fullness of the Gentiles come in to the kingdom of God. James was saying that as they built the Church for the generations to come, they would include the process of the restoration of David's Tabernacle so that the Gentiles would know the Lord.

Probably more people know more about King David than any biblical character other than Jesus. He was a shepherd. He was a musician. He was a composer. He was a national civil hero. He was a prophet. He was a king. He was a warrior. He also received divine revelation for the Temple that his son, Solomon, would build. God provided him the blueprint, which he passed on to Solomon. From this blueprint, once the Temple was completed, the glory of God filled every crevice (see 1 Kings 8:10-15). Whereas the Tabernacle of Moses was for the Israelites alone, the Tabernacle of David included both Jew and Gentile.

1. David's Tabernacle pointed us toward a new covenant filled with grace and faith.
2. David's Tabernacle pointed us to a new Church order, where all believers could be kings and priests. David demonstrated this.
3. David's Tabernacle, after the dedication, shifted from animal sacrifices to sacrifices of joy, thanksgiving and praise.
4. David's Tabernacle became the habitation of the Ark of God's presence until the Temple was completed.
5. David's Tabernacle had the Ark of the Covenant and foretold of someone who would come and sit upon the Throne forever.
6. David's Tabernacle didn't have a veil, so there was access. This represented mediation and intercession.
7. David's Tabernacle had singers, musical instruments and songs of praise within the confines of the tent. A new order and continual sound of worship arose.
8. David's Tabernacle opened the door for the coming of all nations. Whether you were circumcised or uncircumcised, you had access to this tabernacle.

When God says He is restoring the Tabernacle of David, He is not bringing us to an Old Testament order. He is just making sure that everything is shifted from the law of Moses' tabernacle to the prophetic life-giving power that we find in David's Tabernacle. The heavenly pattern that we see now that God is leading us into is found all through the book of Revelation. I believe if we will worship, we will see all that David demonstrated for us, his passion to establish God's presence and to rule as a warrior over his enemies from that presence, being restored to us individually and corporately.

The Harp and Bowl Models

Revelation brings us beyond the model that we see in David's Tabernacle. "Now when He had taken the scroll, the four living creatures and the twenty-four elders fell down before the Lamb, each having a harp, and golden bowls full of incense, which are the prayers of the saints" (Rev. 5:8). The harp represents worship. The bowl represents intercession. As we worship, we intercede and the bowl fills. In *Intercessory Prayer*, Pastor Dutch Sheets writes,

> As we do [pray], the Scriptures indicate that our prayers accumulate. There are bowls in heaven in which our prayers are stored. Not one bowl for all of them but "bowls." We don't know how many but I think it very likely that each of us has our own bowl in heaven. I don't know if it's literal or symbolic. It doesn't matter. The principle is still the same. God has something in which He stores our prayers for use at the proper time. . . . Recently, I believe the Lord showed me what sometimes happens when we come to Him with a need, asking Him to accomplish what He says in His Word. In answer to our requests, He sends His angels to get our bowls of prayer to mix with the fire of the altar. But *there isn't enough in our bowls to meet the need!* We might blame God or think it's not His will or that His Word must not really mean what it says. The reality of it is that sometimes He cannot do what we've asked because we have not given Him enough power in our prayer times to get it done. He has poured out all there was to pour and it wasn't

enough! It's not just a faith issue, but also a power issue.[15]

No one is leading the Body of Christ in this area better than Mike Bickle in Kansas City. The House of Prayer Ministry is blossoming all across the world. Another thing we see is God restoring the corporate anointing in the Church. In Dean Mitchum's book *Apostolic Kingdom Praise*, he writes:

> The corporate anointing is key in present truth and worship. It requires the involvement of the entire Body. The Pastors, Worship Leaders, singers, musicians, arts teams, elders, the congregation, the sound team, and the visual

---

The corporate anointing is key in present truth and worship.

---

team all have a part. All of these join together to facilitate the corporate worship experience. Whether singing, playing, demonstrating, dancing, projecting through multimedia, or functioning in some other form, the following groups are all involved in the service. The key components of their roles in a worship service are as follows:

1. **The Pastors**, as key leaders in worship, bring the revelation of worship and direct the overall flow of the service.
2. **The Worship Leaders** must have a heart for the vision of the house, bring a revelation

for the prophetic, and provide a flow in and out of spontaneous prophetic worship and planned songs.

3. **The Singers** lead the congregation through example and should be ready to flow in the song of the Lord.

4. **The Musicians** provide the musical flow and should be ready to prophesy on the instruments.

5. **The Arts Teams** provide a visual demonstration and example for the congregation and prophesy through movement.

6. **The Elders or other recognized leaders** provide oversight and should be ready for input.

7. **The Congregation** participates and should be ready and actively receiving a revelation of the praise going forth.

8. **The Sound and Visual Team** facilitate the smooth flow of worship by providing sound and sight for participation.[16]

Lazarus, Come Forth!

Jesus came to restore all. There is a group of us who try to meet at the beginning of each year to gain focus. We set aside a day just to pull aside to worship and hear God prophetically. Sometimes we have guest speakers with messages. Other times I lead us in intercession, and John Dickson leads in worship. When we were getting ready to meet at the beginning of one year, one of our elders came forth and said God was speaking to him the following words: "Lazarus, come forth." During our time of worship and prayer, the Spirit of God fell upon John and the following song came forth.

I set my eyes on the horizon in the midst of a desolate
     terrain.
I see a cloud only the size of a man's hand,
But my spirit hears the rumblings of rain
Rise up my spirit, shake off the dust
'Cause I hear the Lord saying, "Lazarus, come forth!"
Lazarus, come forth!
Lazarus, come forth!
Lazarus, Lazarus, come forth!
I'm riding on a new wave, the new wave
Walking in the new way, the new way
Living in the new day, the new day—Oh!
That same Spirit that raised Christ from the dead
Lives in me—lives in me.
And though I stand in the valley of dry bones
The power of God can bring them life—I believe.[17]

What God began to do next was amazing as the revelation of
what He was saying became a song. The atmosphere became
charged with His power and His presence. By singing revelation,
demons flee.

The New Song Breaks the Old Cycle

When David worshiped, he created a new song. We ascend into
heaven, we gain revelation, and we begin to sing that pertinent
revelation to the Lord or the congregation around us. Revelation
5:9 reads, "And they sang a new song." This means that they
responded to God's new redemptive act in history by rejoicing in
song over that act. Miriam did it. Moses did it. David did it.
Mary did it. The elders that John encountered in heaven did
it. They all sang a new song. I think this touches me more than
anything else that occurs. Psalm 20 is a wonderful confession to
make:

May the LORD answer you in the day of trouble; may the name of the God of Jacob defend you; may He send you help from the sanctuary, and strengthen you out of Zion; may He remember all your offerings, and accept your burnt sacrifice. Selah. May He grant you according to your heart's desire, and fulfill all your purpose. We will rejoice in your salvation, and in the name of our God we will set up our banners! May the LORD fulfill all your petitions. Now I know that the LORD saves His anointed; He will answer him from His holy heaven with the saving strength of His right hand. Some trust in chariots, and some in horses; but we will remember the name of the LORD our God. They have bowed down and fallen; but we have risen and stand upright. Save, LORD! May the King answer us when we call.

However, it's more than a powerful confession. Sing it, and watch God begin to move.

In an article titled "Songs of Spiritual Breakthrough," Apostle Jim Hodges writes:

Many are believing for the Body of Christ to break through into a "new thing" in God. What that new thing is we don't fully know, but if it is from God—it will be great! I believe we need a breakthrough so that we will see cities and nations transformed and so that we will witness a harvest of many people coming in to the Kingdom of God. The thesis of this article is: the Church must breakthrough in worship and intercession before we see cities and nations transformed and before we see a massive harvest of souls.

If the Body of Christ does not worship and intercede according to the guidelines of the Word of God, then we will be hindered when we attempt to advance into the breakthroughs the Church and Earth need to see! The prevailing paradigm of worship to which the New Testament summons us in found in Acts 15:16-17: Here the Apostle James quotes the prophet Amos and declares that the entrance of many Gentiles into the Kingdom of God is an initial fulfillment of the prophecy concerning the restoration of the tabernacle of David. In other words, New Testament worship and intercession are to be Davidic. It is not Abraham's altar; nor Moses' tabernacle that is being restored, but David's tabernacle which housed the ark of the covenant of Mount Zion. Moses' tabernacle, which was at Gibeon, continued to offer Levitical sacrifices. There was a sacrifice, but there was no song. The songs of God and the songs of joy were released at David's tabernacle (see 1 Chron. 13).

The Church's worship today needs to correspond to the worship that is going on in heaven.

The revelation of David's tabernacle reaches a climax in the book of Revelation where we see the ongoing emphasis on the Lamb that was slain and the ongoing release of non-stop worship and intercession. Levitical singers, the sons of Asaph, Hemen and Jeduthun, were assigned to lead shifts of their kinsmen in vocal and instrumental praise 24 hours a day at the tabernacle of David. This, of course, corresponds to the ongoing worship that is going on in heaven. Heaven and Earth are joined in perpetual praise and prayer! The Church's worship today needs to correspond to the worship that is going on in heaven which is recorded in the book of Revelation! Here are the songs of breakthrough the Body of Christ needs to sing:

1. **New Songs of the Spirit.** The new song is mentioned seven times in the Old Testament (six references in Psalms, one in Isaiah 42:10). It is referred to once in the New Testament (Rev. 5:9). This should inform us that both Psalms and Revelation publish theology that is sung. Before scriptural trust is systematized, it is sung. *The Church must always sing ahead of its theology, because our hearts must be impacted before our minds are informed.* Otherwise we are left with head knowledge only. Of course an informed mind can enhance our worship once our hearts are impacted! The New Covenant called for a New Song—a new worship response to the finished work of Christ in His death, resurrection, ascension, and exaltation!

2. **Songs of Enthronement.** These are songs that declare the coronation of our King on high! Psalm 110:1-2 is such a song where the Lord God calls for His Son to be seated at His right hand until all His enemies are made His footstool. This passage is referred to by Peter at Pentecost in Acts 2:29-36. Pentecost was the installation of King Jesus

and the inauguration of His everlasting government. In fact, Pentecost fulfills the covenant promises to David that one of his seed would sit on the throne forever. Additionally, Psalms 120–134 are called Ascension Psalms. These were sung as the people of God ascended the hill of Zion and worshipped the King of Israel and of the nations. Church, let's go up to Zion! Let us, through the Spirit, ascend into the heavenly places (Ephesians 1:3; 2:6; Revelation 4:1).

3. **Songs of Harvest**. Acts 15:16 records James' quote of Amos 9:12 which refers to "the remnant of Edom" and a remnant of the nations being called by the Lord. Notice when James quotes this he expands the remnant to "the rest of mankind." Historically, David ruled over Edom and they paid him tribute. Jesus, the Son of David, will rule all the nations and the Church will reap a massive harvest from every tribe, kindred, tongue, and people! (Rev. 7:9). Psalm 126 sings of the harvest coming in after a time of tearful sowing. Church, we need to worshipfully sing the harvest in and evangelistically bring them in as sheaves carried by a harvester!

4. **Songs of Prophetic Declaration and Intercession.** This is illustrated in Rev. 5:8-9 where we see harps and bowls in heaven. Harps speak of worship and bowls of intercession. Our intercession is like incense ascending into heaven which the angel col-

lects in bowls. When the bowls are full, they are tipped and released by the angel into the earth realm in the form of voices, thunderings, lightnings, and earthquakes (Rev. 8:3-5). This sounds like the shaking at Mount Sinai. The point is: when we are faithful to corporately release incense through our intercession, the Lord is faithful to intervene into the situations and lives for which we have been praying! Don't miss this: we find the mingling and merging of worship (harps) and intercession (bowls) in both the Psalms and Revelation. This is the pattern for our corporate worship in the Body of Christ! This merger releases the dynamics of the prophetic ministry! Then we are emboldened to prophesy over churches, cities, nations, and civil governments. Amen!

5. **Songs of Victory and Deliverance**. These songs are the results of the victory of God and His people over their enemies. The Exodus clearly presents this truth when the redeemed and delivered people of God sing of their deliverance from Egyptian bondage by the supernatural power of Jehovah. In Exodus 18 they sing of the defeat of their past enemies, the Canaanites. Their song has historical and prophetic dimensions. In fact, 40 years later when the spies met Rahab in Jericho she told them that the men of Jericho began to fear the people of God when they heard of the Exodus. *The prophetic song put fear into the hearts of their enemies!* In

the book of Revelation, worship and intercession overcome apostate religious structures and beast-like political structures.[18]

The Shout of "Come Forth!" Creates Recovery

We can learn many things from the story of Lazarus. But one important thing is that when Jesus spoke what the Father was speaking in heaven, things began to happen. Let's look at the pattern Jesus gave us. Jesus watched for His key *opportune times* to reflect the Father's glory from heaven. With the Lord's love for Lazarus, Mary and Martha, it might seem that Jesus would have immediately left His post and gone to His sick friend. However, He waited two days. This event revealed His ability to control His emotions. Even friends and close acquaintances could not coerce Him out of the Father's timing. He was not moved to action by external forces. This is key for us in days ahead. Our emotions must be intact to keep us in God's perfect timing. This will ensure that we will be at the right place at the right time. In those days the rabbis taught that after three days the soul returned to God. It was believed that the soul hovered near the deceased for three days. Jesus' delay meant Lazarus was in the grave for four days. This meant he was good and dead, and that his soul had departed. This is the only record in the Bible of a resurrection occurring past three days.

He chose to release the sound at a key place and time in history so that the strongman of unbelief would be overcome. Bethany was a gateway into Judea, a stronghold of religion and unbelief. Look for those key gateways in the region where you live. Unbelief is such a hindering force that it will keep us from seeing the best that God has for us in days ahead. Yet it was in this atmosphere that he performed this powerful miracle.

He revealed the progression or ascent of faith that was necessary for an individual to overcome their unbelief.

He kept working with Martha, Mary and His disciples to show them His character. He encouraged them to believe. "If you will believe," He kept saying, "you will see the glory of God." Our faith level must be raised to a new dimension in the Body of Christ to overcome what is ahead. Resurrection, life and faith have a proportionate relationship that is necessary for us to understand if we are to overcome what is ahead in our future.

This sound caused hopelessness to turn to resurrection power. Martha and Mary had lost all hope of seeing their brother again. However, Jesus kept breaking the power of hopelessness and encouraging them in faith. We must be delivered now from hope deferred! To "resurrect" means to bring to view, attention, or use again; to raise from the dead; the rising again to life. Why did John devote so much time to this particular miracle? Was the

---

Jesus overcame and was resurrected, and in doing so defeated hopelessness in our lives.

---

raising of a dead person the issue? What was the relationship of this particular display of power and the events that were to come? Jesus stated that Lazarus's sickness was not unto death, but "for the glory of God" (John 11:4). This was a culminating event in Jesus' life that eventually led to His own death and to the ultimate defeat of the dark powers holding humanity. Jesus overcame and was resurrected, and in doing so defeated hopelessness in our lives.

The sound of heaven releases power. Power produces relationship or brings division. This display of the power of

God caused individuals to choose either to begin to plot Jesus' death or to shout "Hosanna" and usher Him in as King. The Body of Christ is about to be realigned over the display of the power of God. Do not expect everyone to receive the power that will be displayed in the days ahead. The power of God is life to many, but foolishness to others.

Come Forth and Recover

As we sang this song, we knew that many trials would attempt to overtake us in days ahead. We have seen much turmoil in the earth. We have seen death and destruction. However, this is a season of recovery in the Body of Christ. This new song has helped bring faith into the Body of Christ. Hear the Lord shouting over you *"Come forth!"* This means to escape, break out, bring forth, draw to an end, lead out, to depart from a condemned situation. *Come forth!* Let this shout of the Lord rise in your midst and declare a recovery of what you have lost in the past season. Below is a list for you to proclaim this supernatural recovery in your life, along with Scriptures for you to declare victory in these areas:

- Recover lost and broken relationships (see Jer. 29:14).
- Recover your prophetic call (see Ps. 105:19).
- Recover delayed promises (see 2 Cor. 1:20).
- Recover the spirit and gift of faith (see Rom. 1:17, Ps. 23:3).
- Recover the miracle of healing (see Jer. 30:17).
- Recover your spiritual stability (see Mal. 3:10, Ps. 129:8).
- Recover your financial stability (see 1 Sam. 7:11-14, 2 Chron. 20:6).
- Recover joy (see Neh. 8:10).
- Recover wasted years (see Joel 2:25).

• Recover the lost sheep stolen from your pasture (see 1 Sam. 17:34-37; 30:20).

• Recover the blessings of God (see Deut. 28:1-4).

• Recover all (see 1 Sam. 30).

In *Possessing Your Inheritance*, Rebecca Wagner Sytsema and I write about restoration. We begin by saying that the Lord removes three things: legalism, condemnation and judgmentalism. As we ascend in worship, these fall off of us. We then declare that He restores three things: intimate contact with Himself, our Father/child relationship and our childlike faith. This causes restoration to abound within our lives. Ascend in worship and see your freedom in God restored. Ascend in worship and see your health restored. Ascend in worship and see your joy restored. Ascend in worship and see your position in the earth restored. Ascend in worship and watch the Lord restore your soul. Ascend in worship and watch the Father's heart be restored to you.[19]

Handel's Messiah: Our Deliverer

Ravi Zacharias shares an interesting article concerning Handel and the great work he did. Zacharias writes:

One of the greatest masterpieces of musical composition, if not the greatest, is the work of George Frederic Handel simply called *Messiah*. Prior to its composition Handel had not been successful as a musician and had retired from much professional activity by the age of fifty-six. Then, in a remarkable series of events, a friend presented him with a libretto based upon the life of Christ, the entire script of which was Scripture.

Handel shut himself in his room on Brook Street in London. In twenty-four days, breathtakingly absorbed in his composition and hardly eating or drinking, Handel completed the work all the way to its orchestration. He was a man in the grip of profound inspiration. Later, as he groped for words to describe what he had experienced, he quoted Saint Paul, saying, "Whether I was in the body or out of my body when I wrote it I know not!" Handel's servant testified that on one occasion when he walked into the room to plead with him to eat, he saw Handel with tears streaming down his face saying, "I did think I did see all Heaven before me, and the great God Himself."

When *Messiah* was staged in London, as the notes of the Hallelujah Chorus rang out—"King of Kings and Lord of Lords . . . And He shall reign forever and ever"— the king of England, drawn irresistibly, stood to his feet, and the audience followed as one. Listen to how one writer sums up the impact of *Messiah*: Handel personally conducted more than thirty performances of *Messiah*; many of these concerts were for the benefit of the hurting and the needy. "*Messiah* has fed the hungry, clothed the naked, fostered the orphan." Another wrote, "Perhaps the works of no other composer have so largely contributed to the relief of human suffering." Even if overstated, the point is well taken. The work was based entirely on Scripture. The focus was on the person of Christ. The spirit of a man was enraptured by the holiness of God. A king rose spontaneously to his feet.

The people followed his example. The first performance was a charitable benefit to raise money to free 142 people from prison who could not pay their debts. In the prison of suffering and evil within which the whole world now lives, the same Messiah offers us deliverance.

Come to this Messiah today, dear friend, and you will know the joy of rescue from sin and newfound freedom to live a triumphant life for God. That will be truly inspiring.[20]

Hear from heaven the sound of this phrase echo through the earth: He is King of kings and Lord of lords, and He shall reign forever! Stand and declare this over your life, household, church, city and nation.

Notes

1. C. Peter Wagner, *Warfare Prayer* (Ventura, CA: Regal Books, 1992), p. 61.
2. C. Peter Wagner, *Praying with Power* (Ventura, CA: Regal Books, 1997), p. 185.
3. Chuck D. Pierce and Rebecca Wagner Sytsema, *The Best Is Yet Ahead* (Colorado Springs, CO: Wagner Publications, 2001), n.p.
4. Harry and Cheryl Salem, *Distractions from Destiny* (Tulsa, OK: Harrison House, Inc., 2001), n.p.
5. Jerry Savelle, "What It Takes to Stay Focused," *Adventures in Faith*, vol. 31, no. 2 (April/May/June 2002), p. 5.
6. Ibid.
7. Robert Gay, *Silencing the Enemy* (Lake Mary, FL: Creation House, 1973), p. 9.
8. Oswald Chambers, *My Utmost for His Highest* (Westwood, NJ: Barbour and Company, Inc., 1935), n.p.
9. Dutch Sheets, *Intercessory Prayer* (Ventura, CA: Regal Books, 1996), p. 62.
10. Ibid., pp. 62-63.
11. Darlene Zschech, *Extravagant Worship* (Castle Hill, NSW: Check Music Ministries, 2001), p. 35.
12. Ibid.
13. Barbara Yoder, *The Breaker Anointing* (Colorado Springs, CO: Wagner Publications, 2001), pp. 34-35.
14. Ibid.
15. Dutch Sheets, *Intercessory Prayer* (Ventura, CA: Regal Books, 1996), pp. 208-210.
16. Dean Mitchum, *Apostolic Kingdom Praise* (Santa Rosa Beach, FL: Christian International Ministries Network, 2000), pp. 72-73.
17. John Dickson, "Let the Lion of Judah Roar" (Denton, TX: Glory of Zion International Ministries, Inc., 2001).

18. Jim Hodges, "Songs of Spiritual Breakthrough," *Federation Journal* (Spring 2001), n.p.

19. Chuck D. Pierce and Rebecca Wagner Sytsema, *Possessing Your Inheritance* (Ventura, CA: Renew Books, 1999), n.p.

20. Ravi Zacharias, Ravi Zacharias International Ministries (RZIM), 2000.

CLOTHED
FOR WAR

It is time to rise up and worship
Lift our voices in tumultuous praise
From the rising of the morning sun
To the going down of the same.

People of God, come up and worship
Let your praises ascend to the heavens
Join with heavenly hosts round the throne
In continuous twenty-four seven.

God inhabits the praise of His people
He desires worship to Him alone
At the sound of our prayers heavens open
And we can boldly come to the throne.

As we rest in this place of intimacy
The sweet incense, a bouquet of prayers
Engulf and permeate the throne room
As they fill the bowls placed there.

Let the prayers of the saints fill the bowls
Those who have ears to hear let them hear
The Lord Sabaoth speaks in the thunder
"I AM" invades the holy atmosphere.

The trumpets call all to attention
Hear the Lion of Judah give a roar
The Body of Christ in corporate worship
Receive strategies to come into war.

We are clothed with the glory of God
And descend with our mantle of war
We engage principalities and powers
They slink back and cry out, NO MORE.

The enemy is stopped at the gate
The watchmen stand firm at their posts
The intercessors continue with prayer
And Judah leads forth, praising hosts.

It is time to rise up and worship
Release the fear of the Lord
With praises of God in our mouth
And the Word, God's two-edged sword.
BEV SMITH, COME UP AND WORSHIP

A New Garment of Worship

When Adam and Eve were deceived by the serpent and disobeyed, the garment of favor and glory that they were wearing was removed. This garment of glory was so incredible that it was not necessary to even have the outer garment that we call clothing. They walked in God's presence all day, so they were clothed with God's presence and glory.

God knew that they could not go forth into the next season of their lives with the shame that had come upon them. So immediately, He made a way to reclothe and cover their guilt. A couple of things happened at this juncture in Genesis 3:20. Woman's identity changed. Adam called his wife's name Eve, meaning the mother of all living. God then shed the blood of innocent animals to provide garments of skin. This foreshadowed how the blood would work to cover us in days ahead to atone for our sins. Adam and Eve had made a feeble attempt to reclothe themselves with fig leaves. However, God's plan had sacrifice involved.

Garments are an issue all the way through the Word of God. When we study garments, we find that they are symbolic of an individual's identity. Without worship our proper identity never comes forth. Also, when we study the word "glory" we find that it is an expression of God through us that produces His identity in us.

Jacob passed on the garment of inheritance of Abraham and Isaac to Joseph. That garment was despised, yet God found a way through Joseph's trials to reclothe him so that the posterity of the future of his promise could not be thwarted. Ruth had to remove her garment of mourning and reclothe herself so that the inheritance of Israel could be connected and passed to the next generation. Elijah knew he had not finished what God had sent him to do on Earth, and he passed his garment on to Elisha for the completion of God's restorative shift in Israel. That garment had such great authority that Jezebel, arrayed in all of her manipulation, could not overcome its power.

In Revelation, the Bride (which is the Church) is clothed for war to overcome her enemies.

Jesus, of course, wore a robe of redemption up to the Cross. Then God clothed Him in glory again, and He blew this glory on His disciples. Now the Spirit of God can be seen shining through each one of us because of the Father's love and the Son's obedience. In Revelation, the Bride (which is the Church) is clothed for war to overcome her enemies.

CLOTHED FOR WORSHIP

Lavon and Arlette Revells, two of my dearest friends, live in Georgia. Arlette is a beautiful, southern lady. We were at a leadership gathering once, and she shared the following incredible testimony:

> On June 8, 1985, I was awakened by a heavenly being. I was lying on my back and suddenly became aware of a larger-than-life body of white energy leaning over me. His hands were on my shoulders. "Get up," he said excitedly, "I have something special for you this morning." He vanished as I quickly slipped from under the covers, being

careful not to awaken my dear husband, Lavon, sleeping beside me. I glanced at the clock. It was 4:23 A.M.

I tiptoed down the hall trying to keep the hardwood floors from creaking. I did not want to awaken our two children, Laura, who graduated from high school the night before, and Christopher, a 10th grader. Into the kitchen, Bible in hand, I sat at the table. I started leafing through the Bible. I didn't know what to expect or even what to do. Then, my mind heard these words, "From this day forward I shall supply your clothes My way. I will provide for all your needs. You shall be able to buy clothes for others, but I shall supply your clothes through others" (the first of three directives).

I sat for a while, thinking about what I had heard. Disappointment took over. *Why was He so excited? I need a confirmation. I'll put out a fleece.*

"Lord, if this is really You telling me I can't buy my clothes anymore, please give me a confirmation dress today through someone."

That took care of it. Surely, if God was putting His finger on my clothes, He would answer my fleece!

Lavon and I had planned a pleasure trip to Helen, Georgia, that day. All the way to Helen, I snuggled into my thoughts about what had happened. *Would I get my confirmation dress today?*

Expectancy took over. Strolling up and down the sidewalks in Helen, I looked for a shop owner to lean out his door, look at me, and exclaim, "You're the one I'm to give this dress to." Surely there was a glow all over me. I had been in the presence of an angel! The day passed slowly as I walked in and out of shops. I didn't hear, "You're the one."

Late afternoon we started our 75-mile trip back to Athens. By then I was sure I had heard from God. On the way back I figured out how I would get the confirmation dress—Mother. She was helping at the church garage sale that day. I strained to see the dress hanging at the back door as we pulled into the garage. No dress.

It was getting close to bedtime. No dress. *Was it all just a dream? God, I don't understand.* Then the still small voice spoke, "Your fleece was contrary to what I said. I will supply your clothes My way, and that includes My timing."

Thank You, Lord.

Not being able to buy more new clothes won't be so bad. My closet is full of beautiful things. I have probably got enough to wear the rest of my life if I *have to.* I loved silk dresses.

A few days later the second directive came: "I want you to give away every piece of clothing you have that you picked out."

"All right. Show me whom to give them to." By then I knew something was going on, and I wanted to be a part of it.

I took an inventory of all my clothes. After going through everything, I found only two skirts and a blouse that had been given to me. Three things I had nothing to do with picking out! That would be my wardrobe. *But it would take a long, long time to give everything away, so I had a while . . . I thought.*

One evening something strange began to happen. It was time for my favorite dress to be prepared as a gift. I placed it in the washing machine in the laundry room. I looked down at my dress as tears poured down my cheeks. I felt like I was at a funeral. I peered into what seemed to be a casket and thought about the last time I had worn the dress and said my good-byes. This happened each time I prepared my offerings in the laundry room.

Nine days later I received my third directive. "As of today, you are to wear only what has been given to you." (I shared this with no one.)

I dressed for work that morning, putting on the blouse and one of the skirts. What was once too out of style to wear was now most precious. I looked in the mirror and said, "Thank You, Lord, for my clothes."

While preparing for dinner late that afternoon, I heard someone coming through the back door. I looked as my daughter, Laura, came into the kitchen, placed a beautiful package on the counter and said, "God asked me to buy this for you."

I quickly removed the ribbons and wrapping paper and lifted the top off the box. What should be nestled underneath the tissue paper but a beautiful pink silk dress. God's confirmation dress! Laura bought it with her first paycheck from her summer job.

This season lasted three and one-half years . . . and I never lacked for anything beautiful to wear.[1]

THE REMOVAL OF LAST SEASON'S GARMENT

God will clothe us and express His glory upon us for the season we are living in. I do not believe we can wear God's glory without hearing clearly and obeying His voice. Arlette's testimony signifies this. Not only did God clothe her with His voice and directives, but He then clothed her physically to represent the identity of Himself in her. She looked beautiful in the new identity He gave to her. Her physical wardrobe expressed His identity, since she had waited upon Him. He had reclothed her for the season of war and favor ahead of her.

When God brought Israel up to possess their inheritance, the Promised Land, the first thing He did to prepare them for war was not to check their battle skills. This generation of warriors, raised in the wilderness, had not been circumcised, and it

God will clothe us and express His glory upon us.

was circumcision that was the sign of His covenant with them. The cutting away of the flesh that God required of them represented the removal of the sinful nature that would be accomplished through Christ.

> In him (Christ) you were also circumcised, in the putting off of the sinful nature, not with a circumcision done by the hands of men but with the circumcision done by Christ, having been buried with him in baptism and raised with him through your faith in the power of God, who raised him from the dead (Col. 2:11-12, *NIV*).

The weapons we have for war are important. However, the thing that causes us to reflect God's identity is a removal of an outer hardness of unbelief that has invaded our hearts.

The first thing we have to do is not to check our weapons, but to check our hearts, to make sure that the sinful nature has been cut away by Christ and that we are buried with Him in baptism and raised with Him through our faith in His power. This is where our garment begins to reflect our next season. This releases us into the next phase of worship and war. God told the

Israelites they could not stand before their enemies with uncon-secrated hearts. "Rise up! Consecrate the people and say, 'Consecrate yourselves for tomorrow, for thus the LORD, the God of Israel, has said, "There are things under the ban in your midst, O Israel. You cannot stand before your enemies until you have removed the things under the ban from your midst"'" (Josh. 7:13, *NASB*).

"Consecration" in the Hebrew is *qadash* (kaw-dash), which means to be morally clean. It also suggests that we are to be sep-arated from the world around us. Our garments do not look the same as those of people in the world. That is why Paul's list in Ephesians 6:14-17 contains several pieces of equipment that protect our hearts, minds, intents and integrity. With these pro-tected, we only need one weapon with which to fight: the sword of the Spirit, which is the Word of God.

I love the restorative prophets. Haggai began to prophesy during the time of city rebuilding and Temple rebuilding. He was on the scene with Ezra, Nehemiah and all of those worship-ing warriors. However, the people grew disinterested in seeking God. They also got discouraged because the enemy lambasted them. They actually quit building. The garment that God had put on them when they left Babylon to complete this project was left behind, and they began to focus upon themselves.

However, Zechariah came on the scene about 12 years later and began to prophesy. God had a new administration and a new voice to encourage the people to complete what they had begun. In Zechariah, we find a wonderful message about reclothing:

> Then he showed me Joshua the high priest standing before the Angel of the LORD, and Satan standing at his right hand to oppose him. And the LORD said to Satan, "The LORD rebuke you, Satan! The LORD who has chosen Jerusalem rebuke you! Is this not a brand

plucked from the fire?" Now Joshua was clothed with filthy garments, and was standing before the Angel. Then He answered and spoke to those who stood before Him, saying, "Take away the filthy garments from him." And to him He said, "See, I have removed your iniquity from you, and I will clothe you with rich robes." And I said, "Let them put a clean turban on his head." So they put a clean turban on his head, and they put the clothes on him. And the Angel of the LORD stood by (3:1-5).

This chapter reveals a lot about ascending, warfare and being clothed for the future. We see Joshua the high priest before the Angel of the Lord, and Satan standing to oppose him. The Lord is releasing this vision, not the angel. Second Thessalonians 2:3-4 recounts what happened: "The man of sin is revealed, the son of perdition, who opposes and exalts himself above all that is called God or that is worshiped."

When the people of God returned from Babylon, there was moral and religious impurity within their garments. They had made many mistakes, yet it was time for a new season. Therefore, the Lord rebuked Satan and then changed Joshua's filthy garments. The Lord took away all the iniquity from Joshua's past season. This removed the weakness from him and caused him to be reclothed in authority and glory, enabling him to finish God's building project in the new season.

BE QUICKENED, WORSHIP AND WEAR REVIVAL

God also clothes us with life. Once our spirit is alive to Him, He "quickens" us. What does this mean? Think of a woman who is pregnant. The first movement of the baby inside her womb is called quickening. When the Spirit of God touches us, this same thing happens. That which He is trying to bring to birth moves. When we worship, we usually experience this quickening. The Hebrew word for quickening is *chayah* (khaw-yaw'), which means "to live," or "to be revived." The Greek word is *zoopoieo* (dzo-op-oy-eh'-o), which means "to revitalize."[2]

John Dickson says this:

> Our spirit does one of two things: it dies within us or comes to life. It quenches or quickens. Most of what we do doesn't excite our spirit. Many times as we walk through life our flesh and soul are ministered to, but our spirit withers and shrinks within us. That's why when we get near where the Spirit of God is stirring, we can almost feel our spirit leap within us. John the Baptist leapt within Elizabeth's womb when he heard the voice of Mary sharing that she was pregnant with the Messiah. John the Baptist's father, Zacharias, was so filled with unbelief when the angel visited him, that the Lord shut his mouth. However, John the Baptist, even as an unborn child, was quickened and leapt within his mother. Cast off unbelief! Elizabeth then prophesied over Mary in Luke 1:45 and said, "Blessed is she who believed, for there will be a fulfillment of those things which were told her from the Lord."

This declaration signified the beginning of a new era. This was a rebirth of prophecy. Elizabeth was one of the very first to prophesy in the New Testament.

In Genesis 45:25-28, we find a true picture of removing grief, being quickened and moving forth into our inheritance. This is the story of Jacob, who had supposedly lost his inheritance and his blessed son Joseph. Of course, his sons had actually sold

Joseph into Egypt, and then lied to their father and said a wild beast had killed him. They had brought that bloodstained garment, the coat of many colors, to their father with a lie wrapped around it. By that time God had grabbed hold of the whole situation. Remember, God is always sovereign and on the Throne, even in our bad times.

God had orchestrated a drought and forced the brothers to Egypt, where a strategy to withstand the dry times had been developed. God realigned Joseph and his brothers. Joseph sent his brothers back to get their father.

When Jacob heard his son Joseph was still alive, his spirit was revived. At first his heart could not respond to the truth. This is what can happen when we go through trauma and loss in our life. Many times traumatic experiences cause us to remove ourselves from worshiping God. Wounds, hurts and loss harden our hearts. Imagine Jacob being freed from the power of this deception. He had renewed faith for his inheritance to be extended to the generations to come.

THE APPEARANCE OF PROPHETIC REVELATION IN WORSHIP

For victory, we must first win the war in worship before we go to war. Paul prayed for the people of Ephesus. In *The Queen's Domain*, I wrote the following:

I love the book of Ephesians. I love to study the revival in the city of Ephesus. We can find a record of this revival in Acts 10. Verse 2 contains the key question that changed the course of history as Paul arrived in Ephesus. He met Apollos, who was an apostolic figure in that region, and he asked him, "Did you receive the Holy Spirit when you believed?" Apollos had never heard of the Holy Spirit. He had only been baptized into "John's baptism." Therefore, Paul laid hands on him and they spoke with tongues and prophesied. He also baptized them in the name of the Lord Jesus. This started a chain of events that changed the course of Christian history and gave us a great example of apostolic authority affecting a region after the death and resurrection of the Lord Jesus Christ. We find a great pattern in the book of Ephesians. Paul prayed for the Ephesians to have spiritual insight concerning who Jesus Christ was. He then prayed that they would have insight into the hope of their calling in that region. He explained that they had an identity that was no longer of the world that is ruled by spiritual darkness. He gave explicit instructions on how they had been seated in heavenly places above all powers and principalities. He taught how the same Spirit that raised Jesus from the grave had also enlightened them and raised them into a position where they could have victory over their environment.

Paul admonished the Ephesians to understand a greater love and to be established in Christ's love. He then began to talk to them about their relationships. He actually said to make sure all of your relationships are in God's order. Husbands and wives should have right relationships. Children and parents should have right relationships. Servants and masters should be right with each other in their daily relationships. Paul then instructed them to war against demonic forces that were gripping them and ruling their city. That's what Ephesians 6 is all about.

Paul knew there was a system of idolatry in Ephesus that was linked to Artemis [also called Diana]. She was the ruling "strongman" and she had dominions and powers below her that infiltrated every aspect of society. These forces ruled their economic, government, education and worship systems.

I love what Ephesians 2:1-3 says, "And you He made alive, who were dead in trespasses and sins, in which you once walked according to the course of this world, according to the prince of the power of the air, the spirit who now works in the sons of disobedience, among whom also we all once conducted ourselves in the lusts of our flesh, fulfilling the desire of the flesh and of the mind, and were by nature children of wrath, just as the others." And then Paul makes one of my favorite statements in the whole Bible. He boldly says: "But God."

Paul knew that the love of God could change the course of society for the Ephesians. He knew the mercy and grace of God could create a new identity in this people and that the identity could overthrow Diana's system that ruled their society.[3]

When we worship, we ascend. When we ascend, we gain revelation from God.

When we worship, we ascend. When we ascend, we gain revelation from God. Revelation causes us to know the will of God and break out of Satan's conformity. That is why Ephesians is so important for us to understand. Paul was actually saying, "I pray the spirit of revelation will stay upon you so you can stand against the satanic structure inside of Ephesus that will keep you from coming into the hope of your calling." This was the greatest revival recorded in the Word of God. Worship is the key. That is why right in the middle of the book of Ephesians, Jesus ascends and gives the gifts.

Today, the Lord still speaks to us. As I was worshiping concerning a strategic meeting to discuss how to see harvest break loose in an area of the world known as the 40/70 Window, God began to speak the following to me:

This is a new day! Plant your feet and determine not to go backward. The enemy will assault you to press you backwards. Have I not said, "Without a prophetic vision the people perish and go backwards?" I am ready to revisit areas that have advanced My purposes but retreated at the day of battle. This is the beginning of the shaking of governments. There must be a confrontation of governments. My government on Earth is arising and causing entire regions to shake. I AM restoring and raising up leaders. I AM causing My governments and My gifts to align. This is creating great shakings from region to region throughout this land. This alignment is creating a shift in civil government. I AM breaking off that which caused My Church to retreat from the visitations of the past. Many advanced and then retreated! Now is a time to advance! . . . *From worship you will now move into a new supernatural dimension.* Love and confidence is arising in my body. Do not fear this call to the supernatural. The pharaoh systems of this nation will begin to strengthen to keep my kingdom paradigms from forming and advancing in the earth! Do not fear these systems, but keep confronting through prayer the powers that have attached themselves to the structures of governments in your region. I will make you into a supernatural people who can rise up and overthrow that which has controlled you in the past and will control you in the future. My people are becoming a new, sharp threshing instrument. This threshing is producing shaking. This shaking is releasing harvest. This is the beginning of a consuming fire. Fire must be in your heart. The fear of the supernatural is to be removed from you. Religious spirits and occultism have produced fear over the supernatural spirits. Therefore, they have retreated in their prayer life and fallen into passivity. . . . My will has been activated on Earth. I am advancing. Advance with me. I will lead you into warfare. Many have grown fearful of confronting the enemy. I came to destroy the works of the enemy. I confronted both legalism and liberalism. I say rise up in worship that you might confront. Without confrontation, your enemy, the legalist, will gain much strength against you and narrow the boundaries of your freedom. If you will align yourselves properly and allow your gifts to work within My government, I will guide you like a troop into warfare and make you victorious. *Worship is arising. From worship, you will war!* For a sound of war is coming into the heart of my people. Do not go backwards. Take off the old garments that would hinder you. My *advance* is now in the earth . . . My people's eyes are about to see their supply. Advance is now in the earth. Open your eyes and advance with Me. You will know Me as Jehovah Jireh! You will know me as Jehovah Nissi! I, Lord Sabaoth, will now begin to release a manifestation from region to region throughout this land. Let Me clothe you with *favor* and *authority*! Advance!

This was important, since I knew we had to raise up an army of intercessors and prophetic apostolic leaders to move into a region that had experienced God but was now held by religion. This region goes from Iceland, all through Europe, across northern Asia and to the tip of Japan. I was so thankful God had spoken to give me confidence to begin to mobilize the army of God to pray for these nations. A group of people later met in Hanover, Germany, where we sent 122 prayer teams into 56 of the 61 nations in the designated area.

THE ARMY OF GOD

Worship and war go together. But for war we must have an army. An army is a nation's personnel organized for battle. In Exodus 6:26 we see that when God was ready to remove His people from Egypt and send them to their inheritance, He sent them out according to their armies. They did not really have a political organization but were originated to the will of God and prophetic destiny of each tribe. Each had warriors, and each had a portion that God had allotted them.

There are many armies written about in the Bible. Goliath knew that if he could defy God's people, he would really beat the "armies of the living God" (1 Sam. 17:26,36). If God went out with the Israelites in battle, they won. If He did not, they lost.

Armies were organized in different ways at different times. Genesis records how Abraham called upon his servant and other members of his household to go to war with him. In the wilderness, Moses, Joshua, Aaron and Hur all had a role in defending Israel against the Amalekites (see Exod. 17). In Joshua 5:14, we find Joshua was commissioned by the captain of the host of the Lord to go forth in conquest of the enemies of God's inheritance.

Deborah summoned many of the tribes to battle against Sisera. Some were not willing to go. Saul first established a standing professional army in Israel. He led it at times, and

Jonathan led it at other times. They eventually appointed professional commanders.

New Testament Warriors

The writer of the book of Hebrews, in the New Testament, looked back on the heroes of faith and proclaimed that through faith they "turned to flight the armies of the aliens" (Heb. 11:34). John's vision of the end times included the armies of heaven following the King of kings to victory over the beast and the false prophet (see Rev. 19:11-21). In Revelation we also find that the six angels sounded a trumpet and released the four angels who had been prepared to go forth and bring a level of destruction to Earth. Universal spiritual warfare resulted from this trumpet blast. The army was always comprised of the people of God, prophets, soldiers, heavenly hosts and other leaders.

> Today God is raising up an army
> of worshiping warriors.

In the Greek, the word for army is *strateuma*, which means an armament, a body of troops organized in a systematic way. When we study this word we see that it is also linked with strategy. So an army gains strategy and then moves in order to accomplish victory.

Today God is raising up an army of worshiping warriors. No force on Earth will be able to withstand this army. In the New Testament we find this principle: God had His Church, or *ekklesia* group, called out and assembled together as one man.

This army was called out to complete the purpose of God in the earthly realm (see Heb. 8:1-13).

This group was called to worship Him. They also are called to enlist others. They are established under His authority (see Matt. 16:13-21). They have a sure foundation (see Eph. 2:20). They demonstrate His redeeming death by exercising the power of His resurrection. They know that He is the head. They are members. They fellowship together to gain strength and access the mind of their leader. They are fighting against an enemy and his hierarchy. They are bold witnesses, and they have a hope of their leader's return to fill and restore all things in the earthly realm.

They worship unrestrained, so they can obey and further their master's Kingdom plan. They are a Bride ready for war at all times to avenge the enemy and defeat his plan of darkness. Arise, worshiping warriors! Let the Church arise!

Arise Worshiping Warriors!

Arise, you worshiping warriors
Though small in number you may be.
Arise and take your place
In God's plan and destiny.

Be not weary in well doing
Be courageous as you stand.
In His truth and righteousness
Go forth and take your land.

Raise the shield of love and faith
Lift the sword triumphantly.
God has promised you protection
As you rout the enemy.

Prophesy to principalities
Into darkness speak the light.
See the dead and conquered foe
Lord Sabaoth, with you will fight.

So . . . let the music start to play
Strike the timbrels, sing and dance.
For your Jubilee is here
By His Spirit you'll advance.[4]

Let the godly ones exult in glory; let them sing for joy on
their beds. Let the high praises of God be in their mouth,
and a two-edged sword in their hand, to execute
vengeance on the nations and punishment on the peoples, to bind their kings with chains and their nobles
with fetters of iron, to execute on them the judgment
written; this is an honor for all His godly ones. Praise the
Lord!" (Pss. 149:5-9, NASB).

Worship and warfare are a natural mix in the kingdom of
God. As this psalmist wrote, it is "an honor for all His godly
ones" to carry a sword as we praise. Understand, of course, that
our fight "is not against flesh and blood" (Eph. 6:12); rather, we,
as the Church, have not only the honor but also the responsibility of binding the principalities and powers and executing God's
written judgments on them. What are the written judgments
against them? "The Son of God appeared for this purpose, to
destroy the *works of the devil*" (1 John 3:8, *NASB*, emphasis added).
"At the name of Jesus every knee will bow, of those who are in
heaven and on earth and under the earth, and that every tongue
will confess that Jesus Christ is Lord, to the glory of God the
Father" (Phil. 2:10-11, *NASB*).

Robert Stearns, in his book *Prepare the Way*, writes,

We must understand that spiritual warfare is ultimately about lordship. All authority belongs to Christ. There is no domain free from the imposition of His sovereign will. . . . So when we talk about warfare, the goal of our warfare is not the battle, but the lordship of Christ we seek to bring to every domain. . . . This begins with the revelation that all domains—companies, armies, universities, even nations—are run by mere people. . . . We cannot—must not—we dare not see these people as the enemy. We are not wrestling against them. They are the precious lives for whom Christ died.[5]

We do not war because we are disposed to violence. We war because we are compelled by Him whom we love to bring His lordship to every domain. And, as Robert wrote, we do not war against the people for whom Christ died, we war against the

> We war because we are compelled
> by Him whom we love to bring
> His lordship to every domain.

rulers, against the powers, against the world forces of this darkness, against the spiritual forces of wickedness in the heavenly places (see Eph. 6:12, *NASB*). Though these forces of darkness influence people to do their bidding, we must always keep in mind that our war is not against the people. Even in times when we have to confront people in love, we keep our perspective clear. Though our enemies are the spiritual forces of wickedness in the heavenly places, we must remember that Satan's system is mobilized on Earth through people.

We must not be deceived over how his system is working. Therefore, we can be as wise as serpents in the spirit but gentle as doves in the natural (see Matt. 10:16)—in other words, militant in the spiritual realm, but full of the fruits of the spirit in the natural realm.

> Giving no cause for offense in anything, so that the ministry will not be discredited, but in everything commending ourselves as servants of God, in much endurance, in afflictions, in hardships, in distresses, in beatings, in imprisonments, in tumults, in labors, in sleeplessness, in hunger, in purity, in knowledge, in patience, in kindness, in the Holy Spirit, in genuine love, in the word of truth, in the power of God; *by the weapons of righteousness* for the right hand and the left (2 Cor. 6:3-7, *NASB*, emphasis added).

Our weapons are righteous. They employ the elements of endurance, patience, genuine love, truth and the power of God, which, in the spiritual realm, are mighty.

> For the weapons of our warfare are not carnal but mighty in God for pulling down strongholds, casting down arguments and every high thing that exalts itself against the knowledge of God, bringing every thought into captivity to the obedience of Christ (2 Cor. 10:4-5).

In our worship, we are bringing the lordship of Jesus Christ over areas that have exalted themselves against the knowledge of God. With the high praises of God in our mouth and the sword of the Spirit in our hands, we are executing the judgment written against the enemy of our faith. The earth and all that is on it are God's, and He wants to possess it.

- Behold, all souls are Mine; the soul of the father as well as the soul of the son is Mine (Ezek. 18:4, *NASB*).
- For all the earth is Mine (Exod. 19:5, *NASB*).
- "In that day I will raise up the fallen booth of David, and wall up its breaches; I will also raise up its ruins and rebuild it as in the days of old; that they may possess the remnant of Edom and all the nations who are called by My name," declares the LORD who does this (Amos 9:11-12, *NASB*).

God's intent has been to raise up the level of worship that David established in the Tabernacle to use as a weapon of warfare in these last days to possess all the nations of the earth. The word "possess" is from the Hebrew word *yaresh* (yaw-raysh'), which means to occupy by driving out the previous tenants, and possessing their place and by implication, to seize, to inherit; also to expel. And this is to be done by reestablishing David's prototype of praise and worship in the Tabernacle.

INTERCESSORY WORSHIP

God starts by releasing His burden to a willing soul on Earth who will respond to Him. This burden leads to intercession. Intercession has to include worship to accomplish God's plan.

John Dickson wrote:

It was 1987, and Chuck Pierce had been in our church a little over a year; an interesting fellow, a little strange but likable—certainly a prophet, but not pushy or harsh. He was in a ministry based in our city that smuggled Bibles into iron curtain countries. We could see a depth of spirituality and wisdom about him, but quite honestly, when he shared things we didn't have a paradigm to understand what he was talking about. His Bible was alive in a way to him, where it seemed in our Bible all the revelation he was sharing was hidden to us. Knowing, however, that he was a man of prayer, our pastor asked him to teach a six-week series on intercession. It was on Thursday nights and I had to lead worship for it. Just think of it, an hour of teaching on prayer every Thursday night for the next six weeks—six weeks! Prayer for six straight weeks! Oh my. The thought of it sent me into my own intercession, "Lord, help me, I can't take six weeks of this. I could be home rearranging my sock drawer or something—anything." Oh well, in all things give thanks. So off I went to the gallows of my Thursday-night sentence. Though my attitude that first evening was less than exemplary as a worship leader, my heart began to be won over by this man as he opened our eyes to the call that was in God's heart for those who would do His bidding as intercessors. And as time went on, to my amazement (and Chuck's), I actually began to understand some of the things he was saying.

Then, something even more unbelievable happened—he took us outside the four walls of our church—to pray! We rented the top floor of the tallest building in the city, a financial institution. We had a view of the whole area as we interceded from that high place. The worship that we had been having at the beginnings of the meetings was now being mixed with the prayers all through the meeting. We never stopped worshiping as we interceded. From the financial institution, we went to the seat of our local government. We rented a room in the courthouse to have our meeting. Then we went to the center of our education system. On and on we went to different places of significance in our city. We even ended up in the oldest church in our city, First Methodist. The worship and the intercession gained intensity as we mixed them together.

Thus, the worship in our church took a shift in paradigm. It began to spring from our hearts of intercession, from God's heart over our city. He would direct us against the powers of the enemy that had footholds in our area and held sway over the mind-sets of the people. In our worship we would stand against these powers and lift up the name of Jesus over them. This new paradigm of praise and worship opened the door to the prophetic as we listened for the voice of God to direct us in our intercession. Addressing the powers that God directed us against brought our worship into the realm of warfare. All of these were big changes. Our church had always believed in prayer; we had prayer meetings and prayer during church services and such, but intercession was an aspect of prayer different from what we were acquainted with. What was different?

HE MEDIATES FOR US, WE MEDIATE FOR HIM

To "intercede," according to *Merriam-Webster's Collegiate Dictionary*, means "to intervene between parties with a view to reconciling differences."[6] This sounds like what Jesus did on the cross; He acted between two differing parties—God, who was righteous, and man, who was in sin. This sin had caused a separation, a gap between God and man. Jesus had prayed often for mankind, but intercession is prayer that eradicates a gap;

therefore, Jesus had to rectify the cause of the gap—man's sin. God had declared that the price for man's sin was death, so to reconcile these two parties and bridge the gap, Jesus paid the price for their sin by dying on the cross. This is the ultimate picture of intercession, and Jesus, of course, is referred to in Scripture as our intercessor (see Rom. 8:34, Heb. 7:25). He is the utimate intercessor.

John Dickson adds:

Our own intercession might be on a lesser scale but still is an important part of God's plan. He calls us to stand in the gap between Him and that which He desires to be rectified. As intercessors, we have to see what it will take to rectify it and bridge the gap. Here's an example: perhaps intercessors are gathering before a service, seeking the Lord, praying for the service, the people who will attend and the ones who will minister. As they pray, God reveals to them that a spirit of fear has been loosed against the people, and the congregation will be seized by fear. Fear is in direct conflict with the character of God, and His people cannot function as He desires if they are oppressed by it. The intercessors begin to pray that God's people be free of the spirit of fear. They proclaim the Scriptures that deal with it. "There is no fear in love; but perfect love casts out fear" (1 John 4:18, *NASB*). "I fear no evil, for You are with me" (Ps. 23:4, *NASB*). "Though a host encamp against me, my heart will not fear" (Ps. 27:3, *NASB*). "Do not fear, for I am with you" (Isa. 41:10, *NASB*).

They pray in the name of Jesus and take authority over the spirit of fear and command it to leave. They watch the worship leader to see if he or she picks up on the same spirit. In worship, God begins to direct them to sing songs that would quell fear and release faith. Finally, there is a release, and the Spirit of God begins to sweep across the assembly. Faith begins to arise. Then, to know when their job is done, intercessors usually operate in a gift of the Spirit called discerning of spirits (see 1 Cor. 12:10). By this gift, the intercessors and worshipers can discern when that spirit breaks and flees and the gap between God and His people is bridged. The spirit of fear had rendered God's people ineffective in interacting with Him and receiving from Him.

In her book *The Voice of God*, Cindy Jacobs writes,

> The worship service itself can amount to a prophetic message that God is expressing to the church. When this happens, a powerful anointing will come upon the music. The worship will quicken within the hearts of the people. For instance, if the Lord is saying to His people "Fear not," and a song is sung that proclaims those words, life will spring up in those who are singing. It will give them special faith. They are not to fear, for God is with them through their trials.[7]

Tambourines and Lyres

In one of our intercessory times, the Spirit of God fell and I began to prophesy, "Take your tambourines out of the trees. Take them down, people, and begin to worship." John then began to sing the following song:

> The earth could not contain Him
> and the stone was rolled away
> Death has lost its sting, our Lord has conquered it today
> The powers and principalities are broken

He has risen from the grave
With tambourines and harps will I praise
He broke the power of death

He has risen from the grave
With tambourines and harps will I raise—a song of victory
With tambourines and praise will I sing unto the King
He's broken forth with strength and victory
Christ Jesus is His name and He has healing in His wings
To strike the bonds of our infirmity

He leads a great procession of the souls that He's set free
And brings them up before His Father's throne
He's washed them with His blood and brought them
sanctified and clean
A righteous holy sacrifice to God[8]

It is through the praises of His saints that God springs into
action against His enemies.

"Clap your hands, all you nations; shout to God with cries
of joy. . . . God has ascended amid shouts of joy, the LORD amid
the sounding of trumpets" (Ps. 47:1,5, *NIV*). In the midst of our
shouts of praise, God arises. He launches forth from our worship. "And every blow of the rod of punishment, which the
LORD will lay on him, will be with the music of tambourines
and lyres" (Isa. 30:32, *NASB*). As we praise Him, He begins to
execute His punishment on the enemy. It is our worship that
stirs Him to action.

Jesus in the Temple

When Jesus entered Jerusalem to the shouts of, "Hosanna [to
God] in the highest," He did something He had never done before
in all of His ministry. He entered the Temple to "possess" it. It

was His Father's house, and it had been taken over by money changers and merchants (Matt. 21:12). Robert Gay, in his book *Silencing the Enemy*, writes:

> I want you to see what motivated Jesus to go into the temple and drive the moneychangers out. I do not believe it was merely the activities of the moneychangers, because Jesus had seen them before in the temple. It was not the selling of the doves, for this had been going on for years, and Jesus had never done anything about it. What caused Jesus to rise with righteous indignation in a violent assault against these men? It was the shouts of praise that were coming from the people.[9]

Paul and Silas as Examples

Paul and Silas praised God with their backs beaten and their hands and feet in stocks in the Philippian jail. God arose with such a shout that it shook the foundation of the jail and they were freed from their bonds. The war is always over worship. Why war? It's not a very pleasant consideration or a great desire of most, especially those who are phlegmatic in nature. John Dickson said:

> You could put me on a mountaintop with my guitar and not worry about coming back to get me. I would sit and sing my songs to Jesus and gaze at the beautiful scenery until it was time for the trumpet to sound.

But as we have seen in the last few chapters, when we add intercession to worship, we begin to see God's heart for the things that are a little further down the mountain. We actually see Him wanting to touch the valley and those who are in it—the lost, the wounded and those held in all sorts of bondage. He longs to touch the government, the economic system and the school system. His heart wants to save the unborn child. All of this entails war. We worship so we might go to war with Him.

Notes

1. Arlette Revells, e-mail to author, March 28, 2002.
2. *Biblesoft's New Exhaustive Strong's Numbers and Concordance with Expanded Greek-Hebrew Dictionary* (Seattle, WA and Colorado Springs, CO: Biblesoft and International Bible Translators, Inc., 1994).
3. C. Peter Wagner, ed., *The Queen's Domain* (Colorado Springs, CO: Wagner Publications, 2000), pp. 52-54.
4. Bev Smith, "Arise Worshiping Warriors," (unpublished, 2002).
5. Robert Stearns, *Prepare the Way* (Lake Mary, FL: Creation House, 1999), p. 108.
6. *Merriam-Webster's Collegiate Dictionary*, 10th ed., s.v. "intercede."
7. Cindy Jacobs, *The Voice of God* (Ventura, CA: Regal Books, 1995), p. 194.
8. John Dickson, "Tambourines and Harps" (Denton, TX: Glory of Zion International Ministries, Inc., 1993).
9. Robert Gay, *Silencing the Enemy* (Lake Mary, FL: Creation House, 1973), p. 44.

OUT OF THE WINEPRESS AND INTO THE HARVEST

There is a mentality of increase and victory that the Lord is attempting to develop in His people. The Lord is imparting to us a hundredfold mentality of victory. This mind-set will cause us to see increase and bring the harvest into the storehouse. In Judges 6 we find Gideon threshing wheat in the winepress. Instead of the winepress, he should have been on the threshing floor. The Midianites, the enemy of Israel, had produced fear. They would allow Israel to plow, to plant and even to get ready to harvest, but Israel never could bring the produce into the storehouse. The Midianites would come up and actually rob the harvest. Has this ever happened to you? You plow, you plant, but you never harvest.

The people of Israel cried out to the Lord. That is the first place where worship truly begins. The Lord then sent a prophet to tell them not to fear and that He was going to deliver them. Then the Angel of the Lord visited a man named Gideon. Now remember, Gideon is filled with fear of the harvest being taken and is attempting to keep it secure by threshing the wheat in a winepress. The Angel of the Lord assured Gideon that His presence would be with him and that he could go forward and be a deliverer of Israel. Gideon tried to convince the angel that he came from the weakest clan of the area. Sometimes we rely on our inherent weaknesses not to move forward.

GOD'S GIDEON WORSHIPERS

Gideon could not quite make the shift to believe. Therefore, he asked for a sign. However, he started making his shift by sacrificing and worshiping before the Angel of the Lord. The angel told him to lay the meat and unleavened bread on a rock and then pour out the broth. Fire rose out of the rock. "Now Gideon perceived that He was the Angel of the LORD. So Gideon said, 'Alas, O Lord GOD! For I have seen the Angel of the LORD face to face.' Then the LORD said to him, 'Peace be with you; do not fear, you shall not die.' So Gideon built an altar there to the LORD, and called it The-LORD-Is-Peace. To this day it is still in Ophrah of the Abiezrites" (Judg. 6:22-24). From this place of worship, God reveals Himself not only to Gideon, but also to Israel in a way He has never revealed Himself before. He is declared as Yahweh Shalom, the Lord Is Peace. This character of God would bring about Israel's wholeness, security, well-being, prosperity and realignment. Worship released this empowerment.

However, one more step had to be taken in worship. God required Gideon to "take your father's young bull, the second bull of seven years old, and tear down the altar of Baal that your father has, and cut down the wooden image that is beside it; and build an altar to the LORD your God on top of this rock in the proper arrangement" (vv. 25-26). Even though Gideon had feared doing this, he feared the Lord more. So instead of doing it during the day, he did it during the night. This caused the Spirit of God to release Himself upon Gideon. Therefore, he went from worship to a revelation of God as Yahweh Shalom. And then from this place of peace he mobilized 300 mighty men into war.

THE GOD OF PEACE

Few of us equate God's revelation of peace in worship with a release to go to war. We want peace, but peace at what price? Some think that if we show ourselves to be peace loving, we will never have to war. In 1938, France just wanted to live in peace. So they ignored their neighbor Germany, who was preparing for war. But the desire for peace does not bring peace. Germany was able to take possession of France in only a couple of weeks. It is not our predisposition for war that invites war, it is our possession of something that someone else wants. Passivity does not bring peace; it never has. History has shown us that as long as we are willing to give up what is ours, we will not have to face war. If we give up our possessions, war can be averted. If we give up our rights, war can be averted. If we give our children as slaves, war can be averted. Wait a second, how far are we willing to go here? That is a good question for the Church today. We have given up prayer in our schools. We have given up the rights of the unborn. We have allowed a small minority to determine what is acceptable in society: same-sex marriages; adoptions for those marriages.

We have allowed ourselves to be ridiculed for taking any kind of stand for righteousness. We have not been vigilant and much has been lost. Now God wants His stuff back and He is looking to us to go get it. *But we are the Bride of Christ. We are lovers, not warriors. And what kind of man would send his bride out to fight a thief to get his stuff back?* We are between a rock and a hard place. We can climb back up on the mountaintop and just sing our songs to Jesus (it still sounds very inviting). But how can we now? We have felt His heart in intercession; we have heard His desires through His prophetic words. We have to go out and stand up to the thief, come what may.

PERFECT PRAISE AND CHILDLIKE FAITH

As we set about to prepare for war, let us not allow ourselves to be locked in to old mind-sets about warfare and worship. It is not always about loud music in a minor key. When Jesus was

> God is so creative. He presents us with ingenious weapons.

healing the sick in the Temple (see Matt. 21:14-16), the chief priests and the scribes came against Him, but it was the children who were surrounding Him, singing hosannas. Jesus used this verse in Psalm 8 to answer them. "From the lips of children and infants you have ordained praise because of your enemies, to silence the foe and the avenger" (Ps. 8:2, *NIV*).

God had stirred the innocent children in the Temple that day to erupt in praise for His Son. It silenced the enemy. God is so creative. He presents us with ingenious weapons to war with, and we need to be alert to the strategies He avails us. God is trying to protect the generation of worshipers that is arising. I believe from worship we can protect the worshipers.

We were in an incredible service in Oklahoma City. The worship was incredible, and the presence of God came into the room. I lay on my face, and the Spirit of the Lord began to speak the following:

> This will be a time of determining the authority at the gates of your cities and states. The rulership of the gates is being determined NOW. I am reviewing authority from city to city, state to state and region to region. I have keys in My hand. I know how and when I can release these. I know those who have been tested and who will be used in the future. I am going to begin to orchestrate the establishment of worship throughout this nation, saith the Lord. And I say, as I orchestrate worship and as those respond to Me in worship, I say cities will rise or cities will fall. How My people begin to worship NOW is how the atmosphere will begin to change from region to region. So I say to you, this will be the time of change and how you respond now will cause the changes of the future. As true worship penetrates the heavens, I will release judgment on false worship. Innocent blood has been shed because true worship has not been released. Hail and fire will be an indicator that I AM dealing with those regions who have aligned with Tophet and Moloch and sacrificed wrong offerings. . . . For I say to you, abortion is linked with false idolatrous worship, and I am about to cause a dethroning by the release of My power through true worship. Gather

and worship Me from state to state throughout the land
and I will deliver even those who have not yet been born.
Complacency stops or distorts vision. If you will begin to
stir faith I will reveal how the enemy has shielded the work-
ers of the iniquity in your state. Lawless structures will be
revealed. Those cities that do not respond to My Spirit, I
say the shield will be shifted from them and lawlessness
will manifest in their midst. Cry out for My shield of faith
to be established from state to state.[1]

PREPARATION AND READINESS

Worship prepares us! To win a war you must be prepared. To
"prepare" means to make ready for a specific purpose, fit,
adapt or train. The word also means to put together or jointly
fit, according to a plan or formula, or to make receptive, to
dispose, customize or to equip or furnish with necessary provisions or accessories. This is a season when the Lord is attempting to position and join us in a way for victory. He also wants
to release provisions, so we can endure turmoil ahead and
accelerate in His purposes. One of my favorite Scriptures on
preparation is: "Let your waist be girded and your lamps burning; and you yourselves be like men who wait for their master,
when he will return from the wedding, that when he comes and
knocks they may open to him immediately. Blessed are those
servants whom the master, when he comes, will find watching"
(Luke 12:35-37). The Word goes on to say that He will have
those servants "sit down to eat, and [He] will . . . serve them"
(v. 37, emphasis added). "Girded" signifies a readiness for action.
Those who are watching will have the opportunity to sit and
have communion with the Lord. His anointing will ready them
to go forth in action. This passage is preceded by a discussion
on the heart, treasure and covetousness. No good warrior has

covetousness or is encumbered by worldliness.

Worship gives us confidence! To win the war, you must have confidence! There is no time during this season for self-pity. Insecurity is nothing but pride. The Lord can make you and keep you! Through worship, He develops His identity in us. He is forming "new, sharp threshing instruments"! We do not need to control the forming, or we will rely upon our own flesh in the day of battle.

As we ascend in worship, faith is released. We must war with *faith* (see 1 Tim. 1:18-19). We must be a prophetic people who know what the Lord has said and is saying and war from the power of His voice. Faith comes by hearing, and hearing by the Word of the Lord.

When we worship, our conscience is cleansed. We must war with *a good conscience* (see 1 Tim. 1:19). The conscience is the window of the soul. If our conscience is right before God, the enemy is unable to condemn us. This is where our strength of spirit comes from. We war with *steadfastness in the faith* (see 1 Cor. 16:13; Heb. 10:23; 1 Pet. 5:9). Steadfastness is a different quality than "just faith." You do not waver, and you keep confessing the will of the Lord until a manifestation occurs. As we worship, our faith becomes steadfast.

As we worship, we become determined to see the Lord. This creates an earnestness in us. We war with *earnestness* (see Jude 1:3). Earnestness is linked with contending. We must contend for the apostolic truth that was released to the Early Church and its interpretation to this generation. From earnestness we develop sobriety (see 1 Thess. 5:6; 1 Pet. 5:8). Our minds must be clear, and not passive.

Worship develops endurance. We must war with an *endurance in the midst of hardness* (see 2 Tim. 2:3,10). We must persevere and transfer God's riches to others who can carry forth the gospel. We must war with *self-denial* (see 1 Cor. 9:25-27). The Cross is our victory. We must let it work in our lives to produce the Resurrection power that overcomes the enemy!

THE RISING OF THE ANOINTING

As we worship, our spirit is enlarged, strengthened and matured. The Holy Spirit fills us, and His anointing is released within us. Second Corinthians 1:21-22 reveals, "Now He who establishes us with you in Christ and has anointed us is God, who also has sealed us and given us the Spirit in our hearts as a guarantee." Another way God touches our spirit is through His anointing. There is much misunderstanding of what the anointing is and is

> As we worship, our spirit is enlarged, strengthened and matured.

not. The word is used to explain everything from goose bumps when a draft from the back door blows in on a winter night to the warm fuzzy feeling we get when we hear a well-crafted song played by talented musicians. In the New Testament, the word "anointing" comes from the Greek words *chrisma* (khris'-mah) which means "an unguent or smearing for special endowment," and *chrio* (khree'-o) which means "to smear or rub with oil" and, by implication, "to consecrate to an office or religious service." In the Old Testament it is from the Hebrew word *mishchah* (meesh-khaw') or *moshchah* (mosh-khaw'), which means "an unction," and by implication, "a consecratory gift."[2]

Basically, when you are smeared with oil (which represents the Holy Spirit), you will receive a special endowment and a consecration to perform a service from God. David was anointed to be king. Aaron was anointed to be high priest. Jesus was anointed to preach the gospel. They might all have gotten goose bumps, but it was not because the back door was left open. The Holy Spirit was quickening in them and giving them a special enabling to do what God had called them to do. In 1 John 2:20, the apostle tells us that we have an anointing in us as Christians, a smearing with the oil of the Holy Spirit to do what God has called us to do. When we operate in that anointing as we preach or council or encourage or prophesy or minister in some way, that anointing of the Holy Spirit takes our words or ministry, past the mind, will and emotions of people, and penetrates it like a sword into their spirit. Their spirit responds; it quickens. When we worship, the message or prophecy or music or whatever becomes alive to us. We are able to take the aliveness of God out of the sanctuary to wherever we go.

We are anointed and have access to the anointing even when we do not feel like it or circumstances seem severe around us. John Dickson has a great testimony about worshiping in the midst of pain. He writes:

A few years ago, Chuck was having a conference that I was going to be leading worship for. A couple of weeks before the conference, I herniated a disc in my back. I was incapacitated. I couldn't walk, I couldn't even sit up. I was in excruciating pain. I lived on a little pallet on my living room floor, begging alms of my family as they passed by, "Would you get me a drink of water?" or "Can I have something to eat?" A few days before the conference, Chuck came over to see me. "What are we going to do about the worship, John?" From down on my pallet I spoke words of faith, "I know I can do it, Chuck." We both believed God would raise me up for it, so we never considered a backup plan.

On the day before the conference, I was able to sit up for a short amount of time. This was encouraging. Then on the day of the conference, I got up, walked up on the stage and led the worship. Not only that, I danced, jumped, shouted and had a generally great time under the anointing of God. The anointing literally enabled me to exceed my physical abilities to accomplish the task God had called me to do. When I walked down off the stage, I could no longer stand up. They made a little pallet on the floor of the foyer where I lay in between the worship sessions. My face would turn a pillow white as I lay there in pain. But when it was time for the next worship session, the anointing would come upon me again and I would sing and dance with all my strength. After the last song of the last ministry time of the conference, I walked down off the stage and could not even make it to the foyer and my little pallet. I went down on the floor in the middle of the ministry area in great pain. Of course no one noticed me because so many other people were on the floor who had received ministry. My facial expressions of pain looked much like their facial expressions of rapture. A couple of people even came up to me, hovering over me, saying, "More, Lord." I remained incapacitated on the floor of my living room for another couple of weeks as I slowly recovered from the herniated disc. Why God didn't just heal me for the conference, I don't know, but I believe He wanted me to see the awesome capabilities of His anointing.

In her book *Prophetic Intercession*, Barbara Wentroble writes:

David was a warrior musician. He was a skillful player on the harp. An evil spirit would come on King Saul and cause him torment. David was sent to play upon the harp during these times of distress. As a result of the music played, Saul was set free from the evil spirit. "So it came about whenever the evil spirit from God came to Saul, David would take the harp and play it with his hand; and Saul would be refreshed and be well, and the evil spirit would depart from him" (1 Sam. 16:23). Lamar Boschman comments on this in his book *The Rebirth of Music*. "Note here that it was purely on the presentation of an anointed song by a skillful musician that Saul was delivered from the evil spirit. No doctor treated him. It was not a tranquilizer that subdued the disturbing influence of the evil spirit. It was the delivering power of God that was on the harp David played that set Saul free. David didn't sing a word. The anointing was on the instrument and the music that came forth broke the bands that had King Saul tied to the evil spirit." Prophetic music does more than make us feel good. A spiritual dynamic is released to set captives free. God is raising up prophetic musicians and singers today who are involved in prophetic intercession. There is a blending together of intercession and worship.[3]

ONE MORE STRAW, PLEASE

Sometimes, it is just a matter of applying a sufficient amount of pressure in prayer over certain period of time, like the straw that broke the camel's back. We keep laying those straws of prayer on that camel: 5,983 straws, 5,984 straws, 5,985 straws—don't give up—5,986 straws; then, CRACK! Don't get weary of doing what is good (see 2 Thess. 3:13). Each prayer is a building block repairing the breach. John Dickson shares,

> In worship, the Lord many times has directed me to sing songs by faith about healing, deliverance or miracles

long before I was seeing any of these manifested in our services. Often the Lord has done this through Chuck. "John, you're not singing any songs about miracles." "But we're not seeing any miracles, Chuck." "Well how do you expect to see any if you don't sing about them?" "But I'm going to feel like a hypocrite if I do that. I'd much rather see them, then rejoice in song about them afterward." "But our God is the God who *'gives life to the dead and calls things that are not as though they were'*" (Rom. 4:17, *NIV,* emphasis added).

And that is what He calls us to do in our intercessory worship. He sends us into the breach to sing of His purposes and plans; each song a building block, each song a straw on the camel's back. We sing of those things that are not as though they are, again and again and again, until, CRACK!

LOOKING FOR A FEW GOOD MEN

Is this an aspect of worship that we have not thought about before? It was for me. I always had such a heart to love God and worship Him extravagantly, passionately and with abandon. And God was very pleased with my worship and enjoyed our times together, but one day He began to draw me aside and show me something. He was looking for people who would build up the broken-down wall; to stand before Him in the gap on behalf of the land, so He would be able to find an avenue for His mercy to bring redemption. "I looked for a man among them who would build up the wall and stand before me in the gap on behalf of the land so I would not have to destroy it, but I found none" (Ezek. 22:30, *NIV*).

God's righteousness requires Him to judge iniquity, but His heart is always to redeem rather than judge. He would like for mercy to be able to triumph over judgment (see Jas. 2:13). In Ezekiel, Israel had allowed their sin to create a breach, a gap between them and God, but in His mercy, He looked for someone who could stand in that gap and bring Israel to repentance and avert the imminent judgment. If someone could stand in that gap and break the powers that lured Israel away from their God and pray for their hearts to be softened to hear the words of the prophets so they might repent, then God would be able to extend mercy and restore them. But no one was found. How heartbreaking. Yet we see the same thing in the Church today. Over the past years, God has been raising up a company of intercessors in the earth. Even though the Church still looks weak, and sometimes unstable, God is raising up intercessors who will begin to worship Him passionately. This will steady the stand of the Church and cause us to move forward. Many are still not assimilated into their position and rank yet, but God will do this as we continue to worship. In Ezekiel, the Lord rebukes the prophets of Israel, "You have not gone up into the breaches, nor did you build the wall around the house of Israel to stand in the battle on the day of the LORD" (Ezek. 13:5, *NASB*).

John Dickson explains:

> When Chuck began to teach us about intercession, we heard this cry in God's heart. We began to go "up into the breaches" and to "build the wall around the house" in our worship. It forever changed us. We were ruined. Our reputations did indeed suffer at times. But our eyes had been opened. Our lives were not our own. We were His to throw into the gap. Our worship was His to use as a vehicle to bridge the gaps.
>
> Worship became part of our personal prayer times, our corporate intercessions in the prayer room and a part of our church worship service, though it required a

different mix in each situation. What we did in our personal times of prayer was more intimate than what we did corporately in the prayer room. What we did corporately in the prayer room was more intense than what we did in the congregational worship. We took the passion of our personal time with the Lord into the prayer room, and the strategy of what we received in the prayer room into the church service. The congregation was able to grasp some of the heart of God that we had discerned and was able to enter, in a measure, into the process of repairing the breach. "And you will be called the repairer of the breach, the restorer of the streets in which to dwell" (Isa. 58:12, *NASB*).

When He (the Lamb) had taken the book, the four living creatures and the twenty-four elders fell down before the Lamb, each one holding a harp and golden bowls full of incense, which are the prayers of the saints. And they sang a new song, saying, "Worthy are You to take the book and to break its seals; for You were slain, and purchased for God with Your blood men from every tribe and tongue and people and nation" (Rev. 5:8-9, *NASB*).

Grasp this picture. The Lord is doing business in heaven. The Lamb is going to break the seven seals. He will release the four horsemen of the apocalypse. He is going to have the seven trumpets sounded. War, pestilence, famine—serious stuff is about to happen, and He is taking the prayers of the saints that have been stored up in these bowls and is going to have them brought before Him with worship and praise when He sets about this task.

Be persistent, ask, seek, knock, bother Him, command Him, give Him no rest, fill up the bowls. All those prayers you thought were unanswered or had fallen dead on the ground have been stored up in bowls in heaven. We want quick answers, but there are no microwaves in heaven. These are more like Crock-Pots. You just keep adding stuff and letting them simmer. Then when

---

All those prayers you thought were unanswered have been stored up in bowls in heaven.

---

they are done, they are mixed with worship. And in the midst of this worship and intercession, the Lamb rises up to act in authority and power.

THE EFFECTS OF WORSHIP ON THE ENEMY

In an intense worship service in Ann Arbor, Michigan, after the tragedy of September 11, with worshipers from all over that eight-state region, the Lord began to communicate with us:

A confrontation is mounting in the heavens. Begin to prepare a sacrifice of worship to Me that will overcome the enemy's plan. From your worship I am beginning to mount up a sacrifice of life that can overcome death. A confrontation is on its way. I would have you stand before Me the next 40 days. Stand and declare My name. For the enemy is preparing a sacrifice of worship. The enemy is beginning to mount up with tactics of destruction. Draw near to Me, for I hold the keys to death, hell and the grave.

An ambush has been planned. This ambush has been hidden from you. If you will draw near and worship Me, the ambush will now dissipate and its leader will now fall. Rise up and keep coming to Me. I will be ruler over all. I am setting an order of victory. I am setting timing for victory. I must release that holiness of Myself within you. The time is approaching where you will stand before that which seems invincible to you. My word is CONSECRATE THYSELF! The power of My consecration and sanctifying fire will cause the invincible to crack and you to advance.

I have men and women of faith that I am even now causing to rise up. Come forth, My men of faith! Come forth, My women of faith! Come forth, My children of faith! For I have an army filled with faith! Lean into those who have gone before you and allow the inheritance of faith to rise up. Come up, come up! As you come near, I will neutralize the sacrifice of the enemy! I will cause that which you have put on the altar to become a flame throughout this land. Come up, come up, come up now! Ascend to My throne room, receive My orders and descend with My strategies of victory. And you will go from one season of advancement to another season of advancement. Ascend again! As you ascend I will create you into the image that will create victory.

Do not go from victory to victory without first coming before Me. As you stand before Me, I will transform you into the weapon that I will use for the next battle. This is a lesson that My people must learn now! You are not equipped to withstand the supernatural forces of the enemy that are mounting. Do not walk in presumption.

For I have an armory of supernatural weapons that I am now opening up. I will have a supernatural people that will use these weapons. However, I will only release these weapons through the holy power of My consecrating fire. This fire will form you into a weapon. You will become a weapon that I will release to bring victory in the camp of the enemy. Come up! Be melted! Be reformed! Be transformed! Descend, and then you will have victory from day to day to day. Come up, consecrate yourself, and victory will be yours. Do not try to bypass My throne room to receive supernatural power. Come up, and receive that which can disable the enemy.

The Goliath strongman will taunt you for 40 days. Do not believe his lie. Stand fast. For I will give you the revelation that will cut asunder the power of his voice. Stand fast, come up, and unbelief will not rule you. Stand fast and allow Me to cut away everything that is bringing confusion to you. Listen carefully to my voice. My voice will release faith that will overcome. Stand and get your feet planted. Allow My anointing to arise within you and rest upon you. Some are going to be able to stand more quickly than others. Some are going to get their feet planted more quickly than others. Do not be afraid to hear the enemy's threats. For the enemy will threaten those who are now standing on the wall. He will even entice many to remove themselves from the war and retreat. Therefore, plant your feet and stay on the wall.

Do not reason with the enemy. Do not rationalize with the devil one moment. Draw near to Me, resist the devil, and he will flee. His threats to weaken your stand must not be received into your inner man. For he is releasing seducing spirits to seduce My people from the way I am now leading them. The next 40 days he will even try to discredit the civil government of this land. However, take your stand. There is a present gap that the enemy has access to. There are actually three gaps. I will reveal these gaps if My people will listen, and then I will fill the gaps with My people in the next 40 days. By discrediting My leaders, the enemy will attempt to scatter that which I am forming in this land. For the enemy hates the level of unity that is beginning to form throughout this land. Do not listen to his lies. A lie is a lie no matter how it sounds. There is a lie forming over this land. Do not listen to that lie as it comes to your ears.

For the enemy has determined for this land and My people to scatter. If My covenant people scatter, then they can no longer stand and support My covenant purposes, and desolation will come to this land. If you will stand, there will be an extension of My grace for 15 years upon this land. The threefold cord of evil that would have come in against My covenant will now be exposed. I will expose a network that is hiding in Lebanon. I will expose that which is being plotted in Iraq. I will expose the network that would have destroyed and even pushed in through the Bethlehem area from Syria. And now, because you have taken this stand, when the enemy begins to loose his plan of pestilence upon this land, the pestilence will begin to turn and you will watch the power of its destruction be washed away.[4]

A LONG LIST

So we see the three persons of the Trinity are not idle during our worship. Some people do not care much for worship, but the Father, the Son and the Holy Spirit love it. They get right in there with us. I have only scratched the surface of the ways the

Trinity moves in us prophetically in song. I have seen God bring forth His message in song through the many different personalities of His churches and ministries across the land. There is no one right way. God didn't make us all to have one personality, but one Spirit. I love seeing the diversity of the prophetic gift. Some places use one style of music, some another. In some places the river runs like rapids through a narrow gorge; in other places it is wide and meandering. God uses singers and dancers and musicians. He uses prophetic actions and travail. He uses the old and the young, the great and the small, the gifted and the ungifted, the willing and sometimes the unwilling. And what more shall I say? For time would fail me if I tell of songs coming forth on the streets, in staff meetings, in cars, at dinner parties or while the preacher is in the middle of his message; songs sung as personal words over people in a worship service, during the ministry time, in the foyer after the meeting; songs of comfort, songs of war, love songs and lullabies. God is limitless in the creative ways He looses His prophetic songs in us.

GOD IS SINGING!

So we see, there is a lot going on when we come together and worship. God is singing, Jesus is singing, the Holy Spirit is interceding, and we are looking at our watches, wondering when this is going to get over so we can go home and eat. Paul prayed, "that the eyes of your heart may be enlightened" (Eph. 1:18, *NASB*). We, as the Church, need to let God open the eyes of our heart so we can be enlightened. Just imagine, God in three Persons, the Trinity, is very much a part of our times of worship.

In the Scripture we examined earlier (see Zeph. 3:17), the original language depicts God's singing and dancing as anything but tame. He is spinning around wildly, with great emotion, singing at the top of His lungs. If the person sitting next to us in church did that, we would have him hauled off. But God does it. David did it. When we get to heaven, everyone there will be doing it. I recently told God I do not want to have to make any adjustment in my lifestyle when I go to heaven. I want to just walk right in and be able to fit into what is going on there.

I want to just walk right into heaven and be able to fit into what is going on there.

Mark Twain poked fun of the Church in his day because he could see how their ideas of heaven were so far removed from what he saw practiced in their worship services. He wrote:

> In man's heaven everybody sings! The man who did not sing on earth sings there; the man who could not sing on earth is able to do it there. This universal singing is not casual, not occasional, not relieved by intervals of quiet; it goes on, all day long, and every day . . . And everybody stays; whereas in the earth the place would be empty in two hours. . . . Meantime, every person is playing on a harp . . . whereas not more than twenty in the thousand of them could play an instrument in the earth, or ever wanted to . . . Profoundly devout old gray-headed men put in a large part of their time dreaming of the happy day when they will lay down the cares of this life and enter into the joys of that place. Yet you can see how unreal it is to them, and how little it takes a grip upon

them as being fact, for they make no practical prepara-
tions for the great change: you never see one of them
with a harp, you never hear one of them sing.[5]

This could just as easily be directed toward the Church
today. Shame on us for giving him so much to poke fun at. Our
worship services should be a little more like they are in heaven,
so it will not be such an abrupt change for us when we get there.
In heaven they are full of awe and wonder and majesty. They are
loud and impressive, and everyone gets caught up in them. God
enjoys them. He is comfortable there. We should try to make
Him more comfortable here and open up our spiritual ears to
hear Him sing over us, to hear Jesus singing in our midst and to
discern the brooding and travail of the Holy Spirit.

WORSHIP, WAR AND THE ELEMENTS

The war in the earthly realm has always been over worship,
fought by worship and won by worship. Revelation 12 is a com-
mentary on Ephesians 6. The woman, Michael and the warring
angels of heaven are in great conflict with the dragon.

The woman is the same one referred to in Genesis 3:15, who
would war with the seed of the serpent. Song of Songs 6:4 reads,
"You are beautiful . . . lovely as Jerusalem, majestic as troops with
banners" (*NIV*). Covenant women always bring forth deliverers.
Therefore, the enemy hates a woman who comes in covenant
with God. Not only is she a threat, but she prophetically represents the worshiping Bride that will overcome. The seed of
woman begins warring and worshiping in Genesis, and con-
cludes in Revelation as the Bride of the Lamb.

There are several enemies in the book of Revelation: the dragon, the beast, the synagogue of Satan, Jezebel and the Babylonian

religious and worldly structure. And then, of course, there is the Antichrist, the system and the person. In *The Future War of the Church*, Rebecca Wagner Sytsema and I write:

> The Word of God tells us we are in conflict with five foes:
>
> - **Satan.** The devil and his demons affect most of us, including Christians. Satan has a hierarchy and a horde under him who are confederated to stop the purposes of God. (See Gen. 3:15; 2 Cor. 2:11; Eph. 6:12; Jas. 4:7; 1 Pet. 5:8; 1 John 3:8; Rev. 12:17.)
> - **Flesh.** The flesh is the old Adamic nature that tries to hang on for dear life instead of submit to the power of the Cross. Galatians 5:24 says we should crucify our flesh each day. The flesh hinders us from obeying God. Unless it is suppressed on a daily basis, we fall back into active sin. The devil loves to keep our soulish nature from being crucified. If he loses ground and our soulish nature becomes submitted to the Spirit of God, he loses the ability to use us as one of his resources here on earth. (See John 8:44; Rom. 7:23; 1 Cor. 9:25-27; 2 Cor. 12:7; Gal. 5:17; 1 Pet. 2:11.)
> - **Enemies.** Evil spirits will often become attached to, or embed in, individuals. Then they use these individuals to set themselves against God's covenant plan in another person's life. In the book of Nehemiah, Sanballat and Tobiah were used by the devil to hinder the rebuilding of the walls of

Jerusalem. (See Pss. 38:19; 56:2; 59:3.)

- **World.** The world system is organized contrary to God's will and is being run by Satan, the god of this world. We, as Christians, are enemies of the world. Though we are not part of this world's system, we still live in it. (See John 16:33; 1 John 5:4-5.)
- **Death.** Death is our final enemy. Jesus overcame death, and through His Spirit we can also overcome. (See 1 Cor. 15:26; Heb. 2:14,15.)[6]

Worship overthrows these enemies. God is raising up worship warriors to enter this great conflict.

A RUMBLING IN THE HEAVENS

Many intercessory songs are "not ready for prime time." However, many times God brings forth these songs in corporate worship settings in a way that captures the intensity of travail without overwhelming the congregation. At a powerful worship service in our church several years ago, a spirit of intercession entered into the worship service. Intercessors met before each session and sometimes during the sessions. As we waited before the Lord in worship, the drums began to softly rumble. It was if a storm was brewing in the distance. There was a heaviness in the air. It was pregnant with the presence of God. LeAnn Squier, one of our worship leaders, began to sing:

There's a rumbling in the heavens.
There's a rumbling in the earth,
and the Bride herself is preparing now to give birth.
There's a rumbling in the heavens.

There's a rumbling in the earth,
and the Bride herself is preparing to give birth.
So look up, your redemption draweth nigh.
So look up, your redemption draweth nigh.[7]

The instruments began to pick up the chord structure; the congregation began to sing along. It allowed them to express the weight they felt in their spirit as that heaviness of intercession rested on us. The words were simple and repetitive, but there was such a power of release in them. The Spirit was birthing something; we were His vehicle to travail through. The instruments would pick up the theme and play. The music ebbed and flowed like a powerful storm rising up from the horizon, increasing in intensity as it swept over us, then subsiding as it moved on into the distance.

When it was over, we wondered what it all meant. The Bride is giving birth? It was all so powerful when we were in the Spirit singing it, but afterward we were asking each other, "Is that somewhere in the Scripture?" Then the Spirit brought to LeAnn's remembrance the Scripture in Revelation, "A great sign appeared in heaven: a woman clothed with the sun, and the moon under her feet, and on her head a crown of twelve stars; and she was with child; and she cried out, being in labor and in pain to give birth" (Rev. 12:1,2, *NASB*). Most Bible commentators acknowledge that this woman represents the Church. The Church is the Bride of Christ. The Spirit was signaling that the Bride of Christ, the Church, was about to birth something in the earth and that it was time for us to look up, for our redemption was drawing nigh. Praise God! And we have watched how God has birthed such groundbreaking things in His Church in the areas of intercession, the prophetic and the apostolic that have equipped the saints and opened new areas to evangelism in the earth.

In this chapter, the war is not initiated by the dragon. The dragon is enraged with the Church because he is fighting a losing battle and is fully aware of his manifested defeat. The war is initiated by Michael. God initiates war with the seed of the serpent. Many individuals fall prey to the enemy by initiating their own war.

Michael, the angel who leads warring angels, now wars with the angel, Lucifer, who once led the worship in heaven. Michael, whose name means who is like God, is the great prince mentioned in Daniel 10. He stands as the special protector of the people of God. He is mentioned in Jude as the archangel who contended with Satan for the body of Moses. Of course, this is representative of the Body of Christ.

The Church, God's Bride, needs to hear the rumbling that is going on in the heavens. We need to follow Michael's lead. We are a Davidic priesthood. We are being restored to our authority. David went out to meet Goliath. He did not wait for Goliath to attack Israel. We are to be the aggressor in battle, so the gates of hell will not prevail. We are on the offense, not the defense.

COME UP, AGAIN!

Come up again. I want you to revisit the heights, for I must speak to you again. There will be more revelation at the top. It is essential for your life quest in me. You have had understanding already. Your knowledge of Me and My ways has increased. But you must come up again now. I am going to begin a new acclimatization for you. You must get accustomed to the heights of My mountain. Some days you will not be able to see far. But if you keep coming up you will suddenly find yourself one day with a breathtaking view. Revelation will come like a flood. This is why you need to be coming up again and again. Mountaintop living is your intended destiny. Yes, you will continue to work and minister in the valley, and your work will become stronger and stronger. By your mountaintop visitations, you will be refueled, recharged and renewed through your trips to the heights with me. Come up again![8]

Remember, as Christ ascended, He terminated Satan's access into the Throne Room. Even though we found the accuser going in and out of the Throne Room in the Old Covenant, that was terminated at the ascension of Christ. The accuser, the great slanderer, the devil, is cast out. His case against us is closed! Ascend with Christ and break the power of the accuser. Listen to the heavens rumbling. The Bride is giving birth to worshiping warriors who will defeat the enemy!

Notes

1. Chuck D. Pierce, prophetic word released at Oklahoma Concerts of Prayer at a regional gathering of leaders from a seven state region, Oklahoma City, OK, October 27, 2000.
2. *Biblesoft's New Exhaustive Strong's Numbers and Concordance with Expanded Greek-Hebrew Dictionary*. (Seattle, WA and Colorado Springs, CO: Biblesoft and International Bible Translators, Inc., 1994).
3. Barbara Wentroble, *Prophetic Intercession* (Ventura, CA: Renew Books, 1999), pp. 131-132.
4. Chuck D. Pierce, prophetic word given in Ann Arbor, Michigan, November 15-16, 2001.
5. Mark Twain [Samuel Clemens], *Letters from the Earth* (New York, NY: Perennial Library, Harper & Row, Publishers, 1938), pp. 17-18.
6. Chuck D. Pierce and Rebecca Wagner Sytsema, *The Future War of the Church* (Ventura, CA: Renew Books, 2001), pp. 50-51.
7. LeAnn Squier, "There's a Rumbling in the Heavens" (Denton, TX: Glory of Zion International Ministries, Inc., 1997).
8. Ras Robinson, "What the Lord Is Saying Today," n.p., March 21, 2002.

INDEX